Patsy Beatty   May 20[

I bought this at Hilton Head Island.

THE GINGERBREAD HOUSE COOKBOOK

This cookbook is a collection of favorite recipes,
which are not necessarily original recipes.

THE GINGERBREAD HOUSE COOKBOOK
RECIPES FROM SAVANNAH

Published by Janet Galloway/The Gingerbread House
Copyright © 2000 by
The Gingerbread House
1921 Bull Street
Savannah, Georgia 31401
(912) 234-7303

Recipes and text by Janet Perkins Galloway.
Ms. Galloway, along with her husband Herb, has owned
The Gingerbread House since 1978.

ISBN: 0-9676170-0-6

Designed and manufactured by
Favorite Recipes® Press
an imprint of

FRP

P.O. Box 305142
Nashville, Tennessee 37230
1-800-358-0560

Cover art, *The Gingerbread House*, from an original
oil painting by Essie DeLoach. Ms. DeLoach is a native Georgian.
Her studio is located in her home on a farm near Savannah,
where she and her husband reside. For inquiries, call (912) 858-2364.

Title page art from an original painting by Olivia Jane Williams.

Book Design: Jim Scott
Art Director: Steve Newman
Project Manager: Ginger Dawson

Manufactured in the United States of America
First Printing: 2000   7,500 copies

CONTENTS

WELCOME TO THE GINGERBREAD HOUSE

"Gingerbread" is a term derived from the French word "gingembraz," meaning a sweet cake with fancy white icing. The term came into vogue in the late 1800s to refer to the decorative millwork that many people used to adorn their homes.

In Savannah, the most shining example of gingerbread carpentry is the Gingerbread House, built in 1899 by Cord Asendorf. In an attempt to "out gingerbread" everyone else in town, Mr. Asendorf built a home that has stood the test of time and is now entering its second century.

We purchased the Gingerbread House in 1978 and set about restoring the home to its original splendor. Since 1983, we have been sharing the home as a setting for weddings, receptions, private dinners, tours, and many other special occasions. People from all over the world have visited our Gingerbread House and sampled its architectural, historical, and culinary delights.

This is the second edition of *The Gingerbread House Cookbook*, updated to include old favorites as well as new discoveries. The recipes and menus in this cookbook have been refined over years of working with tour groups, brides, and other individuals, tailoring and tweaking recipes to make every occasion special and memorable. We are delighted to share our home, our history, and our recipes with you, and hope that you enjoy them as much as we have.

BEVERAGES AND APPETIZERS

VICTORIAN GINGERBREAD

The Gingerbread House epitomizes many architectural aspects common in Victorian homes. The home resembles a paddle wheel steamboat, which explains why the style is called "Steamboat Gothic." What distinguishes this house is, of course, the elaborate gingerbread arches and spindles adorning the front porches and side balcony. This millwork, all of which is hand turned, is original to the house. True to the style of Victorian "painted ladies," the home is adorned with 15 distinct colors.

The front steps to the house still proudly display a bronze plaque engraved with the original owner's name, "Cord Asendorf." Inside the home, many original structural aspects of the house survive. Bronze hardware, heart pine woodworking, English tiled fireplaces, tiger oak mantels, and gold leaf picture molding are but a few of the many features that have been in the home since its construction.

To the left of the entry hall is the parlor, a large room with pocket doors that could be closed to retain heat in the winter. In the summer, sheer curtains hung over the parlor entry to provide for a cooler environment. Further ventilation was provided by oversized exterior windows and transom windows over many of the interior doors.

When the home was built in 1899, it sat on a dirt road that became dusty in the summertime. To protect the interior from outdoor dust, a double door with a small foyer was designed. The front entry of the house features a hallway with an oak staircase leading to the second floor. The upstairs floor plan essentially duplicates the downstairs layout.

MENU

VICTORIAN TEA

Tomato Tea Sandwiches

Cucumber Rounds

Curried Chicken Salad
Finger Sandwiches

Pineapple-Cream Cheese Mold

Spinach-Stuffed Phyllo Bites

Strawberries served with
Hot Fudge Sauce

Miniature Chocolate
Peanut Butter Pies

Earl Grey Tea

Cranberry Punch

This is a delicious menu for a bridal shower, baby shower, or other social occasion. Display all food items on a central table with a lace tablecloth and seasonal centerpiece. Fine china hors d'oeuvre plates, pretty cocktail napkins, a tea service, and champagne punch bowl complete the setting.

Sunny Southern Fruit Punch

1 (12 oz.) can frozen orange
  juice
1 (12 oz.) can frozen
  lemonade

1 (46 oz.) can pineapple juice
1 qt. ginger ale

Prepare orange juice and lemonade according to package directions. Mix together and add pineapple juice. Add ginger ale just before serving. *Yield: 1 1/2 gallons.*

Note: Two bottles of champagne may be substituted for ginger ale for a delicious champagne punch.

Sweet Clove Tea

1 gallon water
2 C. sugar
6 whole cloves
1 family-size tea bag
  (makes 1 gallon)

Lemon slices or mint leaves
  for garnish (optional)

Place water in a large pan or Dutch oven; add sugar and stir to mix. Add cloves, then heat until mixture almost boils and sugar is completely dissolved.

Remove from heat and place tea bag in the water to steep. Cool to room temperature, then remove tea bag and refrigerate until ready to serve. Serve over ice, garnished with lemon slices or mint leaves. *Yield: 1 gallon.*

CRANBERRY PUNCH

1 C. sugar
1 C. water
½ C. whole cloves
3 (3") sticks cinnamon
2 qts. cranberry juice cocktail, chilled

1 (46 oz.) can orange-grapefruit juice, chilled
1 (46 oz.) can pineapple juice, chilled
½ C. lemon juice
2 qts. ginger ale, chilled

Combine first four ingredients in a saucepan and bring to a boil; reduce heat and simmer 10 minutes, then let cool completely. Strain, discarding cloves and cinnamon sticks.

To serve, combine sugar mixture, fruit juices and ginger ale in a punch bowl. *Yield: 7 quarts.*

MIMOSA

2 bottles champagne
2⅔ C. fresh orange juice
⅓ C. sugar

8 orange slices
8 mint sprigs

Chill champagne and orange juice. Put orange juice and sugar in blender container, then cover and blend on medium speed until foamy, about 15 seconds.

Pour ⅓ cup of orange juice mixture into each of 8 tall glasses; add about 1 cup champagne to each glass. Garnish with orange slice and mint sprig. *Yield: 8 servings.*

MINT JULEPS

3 C. sugar
4 C. water
1 to 1½ C. white crème
  de menthe

9 oz. Canadian blend
9 oz. standard bourbon
Fresh mint for garnish

Combine sugar and water in a saucepan; bring to a boil, cover and simmer for 5 minutes. Do not stir while cooking. Let cool completely. Add crème de menthe, Canadian blend and bourbon. To serve, fill frosted glasses with crushed ice; fill with mint julep mixture and garnish with fresh mint sprigs, if desired. *Yield: 20 servings.*

Note: This recipe, developed at The Gingerbread House, yields a softer and smoother taste than the standard mint julep, which is made with Kentucky bourbon.

EGGNOG

2 dozen eggs
4 C. sugar
1 qt. whipping cream

1 fifth bourbon
4 oz. Meyers rum
½ gallon vanilla ice cream

Separate eggs. Whip egg whites until soft peaks form; gradually add sugar and continue whipping until peaks are stiff. Set aside, then whip cream until stiff and set aside.

Beat egg yolks, adding bourbon and rum. Add ice cream and continue beating. Add whipped cream; beat slowly. Add egg whites, beating slowly until mixture is smooth. *Yield: 2½ gallons.*

BAKED BRIE WITH WILD MUSHROOMS

16 oz. assorted wild
   mushrooms
   (primarily Morel)
1 large (2 lb.) brie

Fresh dill sprigs for garnish

Clean and dry mushrooms; cut into ¼" slices. Split brie in half horizontally, placing mushrooms on the bottom layer and covering with the top layer of brie.

Bake in a preheated, 300° oven for 10-15 minutes, or until brie is warm and soft. Carefully remove from oven and place on serving platter. Garnish with fresh dill and additional sliced wild mushrooms. Serve warm with English water crackers.
Yield: 30 appetizer servings.

GINGERBREAD HOUSE BOURSIN

2 (8 oz.) pkgs. cream cheese
¼ C. butter
¼ C. sour cream
2 T. chives, chopped

1 T. parsley, chopped
1 clove garlic, chopped
Salt and fresh ground black
   pepper to taste

Cream cheese, butter and sour cream should be at room temperature. Mix cream cheese and butter together until smooth in food processor; add sour cream and pulse a few seconds to blend. Add remaining ingredients and stir to mix. Use as a spread on crackers, or as stuffing for celery or cherry tomatoes. Mixture may also be put in a decorative mold, chilled 4 to 5 hours, and served with crackers. *Yield: 2 cups.*

CHEDDAR CHEESE PECAN LOG

4 oz. cream cheese, softened
4 oz. Cheddar cheese, grated
¼ C. minced onion
1 small clove garlic, minced
⅓ C. chopped pecans
2 T. chopped parsley

2 T. finely chopped pecans
1½ tsp. paprika
1½ tsp. chili powder
1½ tsp. curry powder
1 tsp. dill

Mix cream cheese, Cheddar, onion, garlic and chopped pecans together in a food processor until well blended; chill 15-20 minutes. Meanwhile, mix together parsley, finely chopped pecans, paprika, chili powder, curry powder and dill; pour onto waxed paper.

Shape chilled cream cheese mixture into a log approximately 1" in diameter and 6" in length; roll in spice mixture, wrap in waxed paper and chill until ready for use. Serve with water crackers or lightly salted variety cracker.

Yield: Approximately 6 appetizer servings.

HERBED CHEESE

2 (8 oz.) pkgs. cream cheese,
  softened
1 large clove garlic, minced
2 tsp. minced fresh chives

2 tsp. dried whole basil leaves
1 tsp. dried whole dill weed
1 tsp. lemon pepper seasoning

Combine the cream cheese and garlic in a small bowl; mix well. Stir in the chives, basil leaves, dill weed and lemon pepper seasoning.

Use the cheese as a filling for snow peas, cherry tomato shells, celery sticks or cucumber slices, or use as a spread for party bread. *Yield: About 2 cups.*

PINEAPPLE-CREAM CHEESE MOLD

2 (8 oz.) pkgs. cream cheese, softened
2 T. sugar
1 small can crushed pineapple, drained
¼ C. bell pepper, minced

2 T. green onions, finely chopped
1 C. slivered almonds
1 green top from fresh pineapple

Using a food processor, blend cream cheese with sugar until cheese is smooth. Press pineapple with the back of a spoon to drain all excess liquid. Stir in pineapple, bell pepper and green onions, being careful not to overmix.

Put mixture in a 2-cup oval mold, lined with plastic wrap, and chill 4 to 5 hours. When mixture is set, unmold onto an oval serving plate. Push slivered almonds into top and sides of mold, overlapping to create the appearance of an uncut pineapple.

Cut pineapple top in half lengthwise; place one half, flat side down, at the top end of the mold to complete the pineapple. Serve with plain water crackers or ginger snaps. *Yield: About 2 cups.*

BLEU CHEESE MOLD

1 (8 oz.) pkg. cream cheese, softened
½ lb. bleu cheese, crumbled
¼ C. plus 2 T. butter, room temperature
1 T. chopped onion
½ small clove garlic, minced
Dash coarsely ground pepper
1 T. diced pimiento

Blend cream cheese in food processor until smooth. Add bleu cheese, butter, onion, garlic and pepper; process just until smooth. Remove knife blade and gently stir in pimiento.

Line a 2-cup mold with plastic wrap. Spoon mixture into mold and refrigerate for several hours or until firm. Unmold just before serving. Serve with crackers or apple wedges. *Yield: About 2 cups.*

GUACAMOLE

2 ripe avocados, peeled and
  diced
1 ½ T. lemon juice
1 clove garlic, minced
1 tsp. dried leaf basil, crushed
½ tsp. salt

¼ C. red pepper, finely diced
2 T. salsa
2 T. thinly sliced green onions
1 ½ T. slivered almonds,
  coarsely chopped
¼ C. sour cream

Peel and mash 1 avocado; mix with lemon juice, garlic, basil and
salt. Dice remaining avocado and fold into mixture with red pepper,
salsa, green onions and chopped almonds. Stir in sour cream,
reserving 1 tablespoon for garnish. Serve with tortilla chips or fresh
vegetables. *Yield: 2½ cups.*

MEXICAN LAYERED DIP

1 (15½ oz.) can refried
   beans
¼ C. taco seasoning mix
1½ C. sour cream
1 large tomato, diced

4 green onions, chopped
1 ripe avocado, mashed
2 C. grated Cheddar cheese
Black olives (optional)

Spread beans in a thin layer on the bottom of a 9" x 13" serving platter. Combine taco seasoning mix with sour cream, then spread over beans. Layer diced tomato, green onions and mashed avocado. Sprinkle cheese on top of entire mixture. If desired, garnish with black olives. Chill; serve with tortilla or corn chips.
Yield: 25 appetizer servings.

HERBED CARROT VEGETABLE DIP

1 (8 oz.) pkg. cream cheese,
  softened
¼ C. sour cream
2 T. mayonnaise
¼ C. fresh grated carrots

½ tsp. dill
1 small clove garlic
¼ tsp. salt
1 tsp. chopped chives
1 tsp. chopped parsley

Blend cream cheese in a food processor until smooth; add sour cream and mayonnaise, processing until well blended. Stir in remaining ingredients and process just until mixture is smooth. Refrigerate at least 4 hours for ingredients to blend. Serve as a dip for vegetables or chips. *Yield: 1½ cups.*

HOT ARTICHOKE DIP

1 C. chopped artichoke hearts
1 C. grated Parmesan cheese
¾ C. mayonnaise
½ C. chopped green onions,
  with tops

½ tsp. garlic salt
½ tsp. white pepper
Paprika

Preheat oven to 350°. Combine all ingredients except paprika, mixing gently. Spread in a 1½-quart baking dish and sprinkle with paprika. Bake for 20-25 minutes or until hot and bubbly.

Serve warm as a dip with chips or raw vegetables. Triscuits and Wheat Thins are especially good with this dip. *Yield: 3 cups.*

SOUR CREAM SPINACH DIP

1 whole loaf bread
(round or oval
shaped)
1 (10 oz.) pkg. frozen,
chopped spinach
16 oz. sour cream

1 envelope (.7 oz.) Italian
dressing mix
½ C. thinly sliced green
onions, chopped
1 (3 oz.) jar chopped pimiento,
drained

Using a sharp bread knife, cut around bread, hollowing to make a
shell with approximately 1" remaining around edges. Set aside.

Thaw and drain spinach, squeezing out all excess moisture. Mix
remaining ingredients together with spinach; refrigerate at least
2 hours.

To serve, place spinach dip in hollowed out bread; garnish with
cucumbers, red pepper slivers or other colorful vegetable. Serve
with brittle bread (see recipe, p.126), crackers or vegetables.
Yield: 3½ cups.

SPINACH-STUFFED PHYLLO BITES

1 (10 oz.) pkg. frozen chopped
spinach, thawed
2 (8 oz.) pkgs. cream cheese,
softened
¼ tsp. instant garlic powder

¼ C. sour cream
1 envelope Lipton onion
soup mix
3 pkgs. phyllo pastry cups
(15 cups per pkg.)

Squeeze liquid from spinach; mix with cream cheese. Add garlic
powder, sour cream and onion soup mix. Heat all on stove top over
low flame, stirring until well blended.

Place phyllo cups on ungreased baking sheet; fill each with a
heaping teaspoon of spinach mixture. Bake in 325° oven until filling
and phyllo cups are warm, about 7-10 minutes. Serve immediately.
Yield: 45 appetizers.

CUCUMBER ROUNDS

2 long cucumbers
1 loaf white or wheat bread
1 C. mayonnaise
6 T. sour cream

3 T. grated onion
Dash garlic powder
Paprika
Green olives (optional)

Score cucumbers with a fork and slice thin (20 slices per cucumber). Remove crust from bread and cut bread into rounds with small biscuit cutter.

Combine mayonnaise, sour cream, grated onion and garlic powder; spread each round of bread with this mixture, topping with a cucumber slice. Sprinkle cucumber with paprika; garnish with sliced olive. *Yield: 40 appetizers.*

ASPARAGUS IN PROSCIUTTO

2 lbs. fresh asparagus
1 (3 oz.) pkg. cream cheese
1 tsp. Worcestershire sauce

¼ tsp. garlic salt
½ lb. prosciutto, sliced thin

Trim hard ends off asparagus stems; blanch asparagus in boiling water for 2 minutes, then rinse immediately under cold water. Set aside.

Mix cream cheese, Worcestershire sauce and garlic salt until well blended. Spread thin layer of cream cheese mixture on one slice prosciutto. Place center of asparagus spear near end of prosciutto, rolling prosciutto to wrap around the asparagus. Repeat for remaining asparagus; chill before serving.
Yield: Approximately 30 appetizer servings.

PERUVIAN MARINATED MUSHROOMS

1 lb. mushrooms
½ C. flavored red wine vinegar
   (raspberry is good)
½ C. olive oil
1 clove garlic, crushed
½ tsp. dried oregano

½ tsp. dried thyme leaves
¼ tsp. pepper
¼ tsp. paprika
½ tsp. salt
1 small onion, thinly sliced

Steam mushrooms in boiling water for 30 seconds; drain, cover with cold water and drain again. Mix all other ingredients together in a bowl, then add mushrooms. Store in tightly sealed container and chill 24 hours. *Yield: About 20 appetizers.*

SAUSAGE-STUFFED MUSHROOMS

36 medium mushrooms
¼ C. butter, melted
½ lb. bulk sausage
1 medium onion, finely
   chopped

¼ C. sherry
½ C. fine bread crumbs
3 T. fresh parsley, minced
½ tsp. thyme
3 T. half and half

Remove mushroom stems and chop to make ¼ cup. Brush mushroom caps with butter.

In a skillet, sauté sausage and onion; drain and return mixture to pan. Add mushroom stems and sherry, then cook over medium-high heat until liquid has evaporated.

Remove from heat and add remaining ingredients. Fill mushroom caps with mixture. Bake at 350° for 10 minutes; serve immediately. *Yield: 3 dozen.*

CRAB-STUFFED MUSHROOMS

20 medium mushrooms
¼ C. butter, melted
¼ C. chopped celery
1 T. finely chopped onion
1 clove garlic, crushed
¼ C. butter

4 oz. crab meat
½ tsp. Worcestershire sauce
1 egg, beaten
Salt and pepper to taste
¼ C. bread crumbs

Remove mushroom stems; chop to make ½ cup. Brush caps with melted butter and set aside. Sauté mushroom stems, celery, onion and garlic in butter until stems are tender. Remove from heat; add remaining ingredients. Fill caps with mixture; bake in 350° oven 10-12 minutes; serve immediately. *Yield: 20 appetizers.*

TACO SALSA SURPRISES

1 lb. lean ground beef
2 T. taco seasoning mix
2 T. ice water
2 T. taco sauce
2 oz. chopped ripe olives

1 C. shredded Cheddar cheese
1 C. sour cream
¾ C. tortilla chips, coarsely
  crushed

Preheat oven to 425°. In a medium bowl, mix beef, taco seasoning mix and ice water with hands. Press into bottom and sides of 1" miniature muffin cups, forming a shell.

In a small bowl, mix taco sauce, olives, cheese, sour cream and tortilla chips. Place a heaping teaspoon of filling in each shell, mounding slightly. Bake 7-8 minutes; remove from pan using the tip of a knife. Serve hot. *Yield: About 3 dozen.*

TENDERLOIN TIDBITS

¼ C. garlic oil
1 tsp. salt

2 tsp. cracked black pepper
5 lbs. whole beef tenderloin

Preheat oven to 350°. Rub garlic oil, salt and pepper into tenderloin. Sear the tenderloin in a hot skillet until browned on all sides.

Place fat side down in baking pan. Cook 30-35 minutes, or until meat thermometer registers 150° (for medium rare).

Remove from oven; cool to room temperature and cut into ¾" cubes. Top with warm Béarnaise Sauce (see recipe, p. 60) and serve as an appetizer. *Yield: Approximately 100 cubes*.

SIRLOIN TERIYAKI

2 lbs. sirloin, cooked rare and
   cut into ¼" thick slices
¾ C. pineapple juice
¾ C. soy sauce
2 T. honey

1 clove garlic, peeled and
   mashed
Fresh cracked black pepper
   to taste
36 (6") bamboo skewers

Cut steak into 1" x 3" strips. Combine pineapple juice, soy sauce, honey, garlic and pepper; mix well. Add sirloin and marinate for 1-2 hours in the refrigerator.

Thread beef slices onto skewers; serve chilled or at room temperature. *Yield: 3 dozen.*

Note. These look great on a round serving tray lined with lettuce with a half pineapple in the center. To display, stick the end of each skewer into the pineapple, moving around the tray to distribute evenly.

SESAME APPETIZER MEATBALLS

1 lb. ground beef
⅔ C. minced onion
½ C. soft bread crumbs
1 egg
¼ C. milk

½ tsp. salt
⅛ tsp. pepper
1 T. plus 1 tsp. Worcestershire
    sauce
2 C. beef broth

Combine all ingredients except beef broth. Mix well and shape into 1" meatballs; bake in 325° oven for 20 minutes or until lightly browned. Drain in colander, then simmer on stove top in beef broth for 10 minutes or until cooked through. Serve with Sesame Seed Sauce (recipe follows). *Yield: 3 dozen.*

SESAME SEED SAUCE

2 T. butter
2 T. flour
¼ tsp. salt
Dash cayenne pepper
½ C. beef broth

1 tsp. soy sauce
1 tsp. Worcestershire sauce
2 T. sesame seeds, toasted
1 C. sour cream, room
    temperature

In a saucepan, melt butter over medium heat. Blend in flour, salt and cayenne pepper. Heat, stirring, until bubbly. Add broth all at once and cook, stirring, until sauce thickens. Stir in soy sauce, Worcestershire sauce and sesame seeds.

Empty sour cream into medium bowl; gradually add sauce, stirring constantly. Return sauce to pan, fold in meatballs and heat gently to serving temperature. Serve from chafing dish with toothpicks. *Yield: 1½ cups.*

Italian Sausage Phyllo Bites

1 lb. Italian sausage, cooked,
  drained and crumbled
1 C. heavy cream
¼ C. Dijon mustard

½ tsp. nutmeg
4 doz. miniature pastry
  puff cups

Brown sausage in a skillet, breaking up meat as it browns. Drain grease and crumble sausage; return sausage to skillet and add cream, mustard and nutmeg. Simmer, stirring constantly, until cream thickens; cool

Place miniature pastry puff cups on a baking sheet; fill each with 1 heaping teaspoon of sausage mixture. Bake at 350° for 7-10 minutes or until filling and cups are warm; serve hot. *Yield: 4 dozen.*

Sausage Meatballs in Barbecue Sauce

4 lbs. bulk sausage
2 C. herb-seasoned stuffing
4 eggs

1 recipe Special Barbecue
  Sauce (page 59)

Combine sausage, stuffing and eggs in a large bowl; mix well and shape into 1" balls. Place on ungreased baking sheet and cook in preheated 350° oven for 20-25 minutes or until browned. Drain on paper towels.

Serve meatballs with Special Barbecue Sauce. To serve, add meatballs to sauce, warm gently and place in a chafing dish. *Yield: 6 dozen.*

SMOKED COCKTAIL SAUSAGES

1 (48 oz.) pkg. miniature
   smoked cocktail sausages
2 C. catsup

¼ C. soy sauce
¼ C. red wine vinegar
¼ C. packed brown sugar

Remove cocktail sausages from package; drain well and set aside.
Mix together catsup, soy sauce, red wine vinegar and brown sugar;
cook over low heat for 15 minutes until thick and bubbly. Add
cocktail sausages, heat until warm and serve.
Yield: 25 appetizer servings.

ITALIAN SAUSAGE CRESCENT ROLL WRAPS

4 large links (1" diameter,
   6" length) Italian sausage

1 (8 oz.) can refrigerator
   crescent dinner rolls

Cook the sausage in a skillet; drain well. Separate roll dough into
4 rectangles, pressing perforations to seal. Place a sausage link
lengthwise on each rectangle and roll up, making sure all of sausage
is covered with dough. Firmly seal edges of dough.

Cut each roll-up crosswise into ¾" pieces, pinching dough to
secure around edges. Place on lightly greased baking sheet. Bake
in a preheated 375° oven for 10-12 minutes until lightly browned.
Serve immediately. *Yield: 32 pieces.*

STUFFED SALAMI CONES

1 lb. hard salami, sliced thin
Round toothpicks (about 50)
1 (8 oz.) pkg. cream cheese,
  softened

2 T. chives
¼ tsp. ground garlic

Roll each slice of salami into conical shape, securing each cone on the side with a toothpick.

Mix together cream cheese, chives and garlic until well blended. Fill a pastry bag with the cream cheese mixture, then pipe filling into each salami cone until cone is filled to the brim. Chill and serve as hors d'oeuvres. *Yield: About 50.*

CHICKEN NUGGETS ITALIANO

8 whole, boneless chicken
  breasts
4 C. dry bread crumbs, finely
  crushed

2 C. Parmesan cheese, grated
1 T. salt
½ C. dry Italian seasoning
2 C. butter, melted

Cut chicken into bite-size pieces (1" to 1½" each). Combine bread crumbs, cheese, salt and Italian seasoning; mix well. Dip chicken pieces in melted butter, then coat with bread crumb mixture.

Place in a single layer on lightly greased baking sheet. Bake at 450° for 20 minutes or until lightly browned on top. Serve with honey mustard sauce (see recipe, p. 58). *Yield: 75-80 pieces.*

HOT SPICY CHICKEN WINGS

2 sticks butter
1 (24 oz.) bottle Texas Pete's
   hot wings sauce

4 dozen chicken wings
Salt and pepper

Preheat oven to 450°. Melt butter in small saucepan over low heat. Remove from heat and add hot sauce; pour mixture into a medium bowl.

Dip each chicken wing in the butter/hot sauce mixture. Place on a greased baking sheet. Repeat with remaining wings, then sprinkle entire pan lightly with salt and pepper. Bake until wings are brown, about 25-30 minutes. *Yield: 4 dozen.*

SAVANNAH SHRIMP DIP

2 lbs. shrimp, cooked, peeled
   and deveined
2 (8 oz.) pkgs. cream cheese,
   softened
⅔ C. mayonnaise

1 medium onion, finely
   chopped
2 tsp. prepared mustard
Dash Tabasco

Coarsely chop shrimp and combine with remaining ingredients, mixing in order given. Chill several hours for flavors to blend. Serve with water crackers or melba toast. *Yield: 4 cups.*

MARINATED SHRIMP AND SNOW PEAS

1 lb. shrimp (18-20 count)
1 T. Dijon mustard
¼ C. white wine vinegar
¼ tsp. salt
Freshly ground black pepper
   to taste

1½ C. olive oil
20 snow peas (about ½ lb.)
Salt to taste
Round toothpicks

Cook, peel and devein shrimp, leaving tails on. Set aside to chill.

Make a marinade by whisking mustard and wine vinegar together in a small bowl. Stir in ¼ teaspoon salt and pepper. Gradually add olive oil, whisking constantly while adding.

Pour marinade over shrimp and let stand, refrigerated, for 1-2 hours. Drain marinade.

Trim snow peas; blanch by cooking in boiling salted water for 2 minutes. Drain immediately and rinse with cold water.

To assemble hors d'oeuvres, wrap a snow pea around the center of each shrimp, overlapping ends of the snow pea. Secure each snow pea with a toothpick inserted through the shrimp.

Arrange on a platter and refrigerate until ready to serve. Just before serving, drizzle some of the marinade over the shrimp.
Yield: 18-20 appetizers.

CREAMY SHRIMP ON BAGUETTES

1 (20") French baguette
2 T. olive oil
1 (8 oz.) pkg. cream cheese, softened
½ C. mayonnaise
2 T. Dijon mustard
1 lb. cooked shrimp, peeled, deveined and coarsely chopped

½ C. minced green onions
1½ T. chopped fresh dill
1 tsp. grated lemon peel
Salt and pepper to taste
Chopped fresh parsley for garnish

Preheat broiler. Cut baguette diagonally into 40 half-inch slices. Lightly brush 1 side of each baguette slice with olive oil and arrange on 2 baking sheets. Broil until lightly toasted, about 1 minute.

Beat cream cheese, mayonnaise and mustard in electric mixer until well blended. Add shrimp, green onions, dill and lemon peel, then season with salt and pepper.

Spread 1 tablespoon shrimp mixture on each toast slice. Arrange on baking sheets; broil until shrimp mixture begins to brown, about 2 minutes. Top with parsley. Serve immediately.
Yield: 40 appetizers.

Note: These can also be served cold; simply omit broiling the shrimp.

DIJON CRAB DIP

1 (8 oz.) pkg. cream cheese
3 T. mayonnaise
2 T. dry sherry
1 tsp. Dijon mustard

½ tsp. sugar
¼ tsp. salt
½ lb. crab meat

In a saucepan over low heat, soften cream cheese, stirring until smooth. Add mayonnaise, sherry, mustard, sugar and salt. Cook, stirring, until blended and heated through. Stir in crab meat and keep warm. Serve with crackers or corn chips.

This dip can be chilled and used to fill pastry puffs. Will keep 2-3 days in refrigerator. *Yield: 2 cups.*

SAVANNAH CRAB SPREAD

24 oz. cream cheese, softened
3 T. Worcestershire sauce
2 T. lemon juice
3 T. mayonnaise
Pinch garlic salt

1 small onion, grated
1 (12 oz.) bottle cocktail sauce
1 lb. fresh or pasteurized
    canned crab meat
¼ C. fresh chopped parsley

Combine cream cheese, Worcestershire sauce, lemon juice, mayonnaise, garlic salt and onion. Spread over bottom of a 9" x 13" serving platter. Cover with cocktail sauce and top with crab meat. Sprinkle with chopped parsley and serve with butter or water crackers. *Yield: 30 appetizer servings.*

Sweet Orange Pecans

1 C. sugar   4 to 5 C. pecan halves
⅓ C. orange juice concentrate,
   undiluted

Combine sugar and orange juice concentrate in a large saucepan over medium heat. Stir until liquid is clear and sugar is absorbed into juice. Leaving heat on, add pecan halves and stir until liquid is absorbed.

Spread on waxed paper and dry several hours or overnight. Store in an airtight container until ready for use. *Yield: 4-5 cups.*

Oven-Roasted Salted Pecans

1 egg white   1 T. salt
6 to 8 C. pecan halves

Beat egg white on high speed with electric mixer until stiff. Pour pecans into a large bowl, add egg white and stir until pecans are thoroughly coated and egg white is absorbed. Add salt and stir to distribute evenly among pecans.

Spread pecans evenly on two baking sheets. Bake for 30 minutes in a preheated, 300° oven, being careful not to overcook. Cool; store in an airtight container until ready to serve. May be frozen for later use. *Yield: 6-8 cups.*

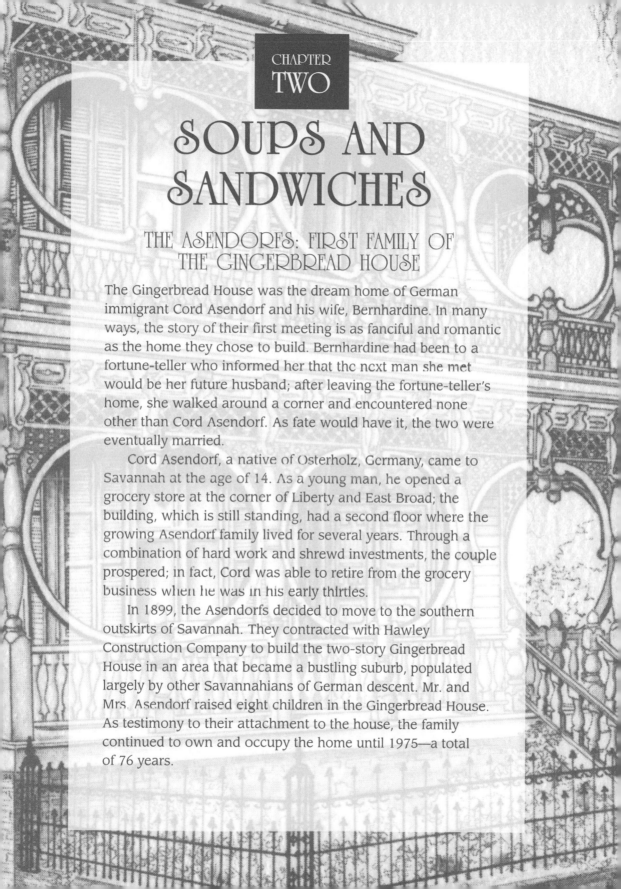

SOUPS AND SANDWICHES

THE ASENDORFS: FIRST FAMILY OF THE GINGERBREAD HOUSE

The Gingerbread House was the dream home of German immigrant Cord Asendorf and his wife, Bernhardine. In many ways, the story of their first meeting is as fanciful and romantic as the home they chose to build. Bernhardine had been to a fortune-teller who informed her that the next man she met would be her future husband; after leaving the fortune-teller's home, she walked around a corner and encountered none other than Cord Asendorf. As fate would have it, the two were eventually married.

Cord Asendorf, a native of Osterholz, Germany, came to Savannah at the age of 14. As a young man, he opened a grocery store at the corner of Liberty and East Broad; the building, which is still standing, had a second floor where the growing Asendorf family lived for several years. Through a combination of hard work and shrewd investments, the couple prospered; in fact, Cord was able to retire from the grocery business when he was in his early thirties.

In 1899, the Asendorfs decided to move to the southern outskirts of Savannah. They contracted with Hawley Construction Company to build the two-story Gingerbread House in an area that became a bustling suburb, populated largely by other Savannahians of German descent. Mr. and Mrs. Asendorf raised eight children in the Gingerbread House. As testimony to their attachment to the house, the family continued to own and occupy the home until 1975—a total of 76 years.

MENU

SEASIDE SOUP AND SANDWICH BUFFET

She-Crab Soup

Savannah Gumbo

Deviled Crab

Creamy Shrimp on Baguettes

Crab Salad on Croissants

Low Country Cornbread

Brittle Bread

Toasted Coconut Pies

Savannah Pralines

Sweet Clove Tea

Place all on a buffet table and let your guests serve themselves. For added regional flavor, prepare Marinated Vidalia Onion Salad. Serve with a light butter cracker as an hors d'oeuvre, or on a bed of lettuce as a salad. Makes a mild textural contrast to the soups and sandwiches on the menu.

SHRIMP BISQUE

1 lb. shrimp, boiled and peeled	2 tsp. salt
¼ C. butter	1 T. lemon juice
¼ C. flour	½ tsp. Tabasco
2 C. milk	Dash white pepper
2 C. half and half	⅓ C. sherry

Chop shrimp in food processor; set aside. Combine butter and flour in saucepan. Add milk, half and half and salt. Cook, stirring constantly, until thickened. Add lemon juice, Tabasco and pepper. Stir in shrimp and sherry. Serve hot. *Yield: 4 servings.*

SHE-CRAB SOUP

1 medium onion, diced small	1 T. Worcestershire sauce
1 stalk celery, diced small	⅔ C. flour
1 clove garlic, chopped	2 qt. heavy cream
8 oz. butter	1 lb. lump crab meat
3 T. lobster base	1 pt. milk (optional)
1 C. sherry	White pepper (optional)
2 tsp. Tabasco	

In a medium saucepan, sauté onion, celery and garlic in melted butter over medium heat; add lobster base, sherry and Tabasco. Mix in Worcestershire sauce and flour and cook to a thick paste. Add cream slowly and mix well. Cook 35 minutes over low heat, then add crab meat and cook for 30 minutes more. If soup is too thick, add milk. Adjust seasoning with white pepper. *Yield: 2½-3 quarts.*

CHEDDAR JACK CHEESE SOUP

2 large carrots, peeled
1 small onion, peeled
1 small apple, cored
3 small jalapeno chilies,
    seeded
3 T. butter
2 C. chicken stock or canned
    broth
½ C. dry white wine
6 T. all-purpose flour

2 C. milk
6 oz. Cheddar cheese,
    shredded
6 oz. Monterey Jack cheese,
    shredded
Salt and pepper to taste
¼ C. cilantro
2 small plum tomatoes, seeded
    and diced, for garnish

Cut carrots, onion and apple into 1" pieces. Using food processor, process carrots, onion, apple and chilies until finely minced.

Melt butter in large saucepan over medium-low heat. Add contents of processor and cook until softened, stirring occasionally, about 8 minutes. Add chicken stock and wine and bring to a boil. Reduce heat, cover and simmer gently until vegetables are very soft, about 30 minutes.

Puree vegetable mixture until very smooth, about 2 minutes. Press through fine strainer into bowl. Place flour in large bowl. Gradually whisk in half of milk. Add vegetable mixture and remaining milk. Return to the saucepan; cook over medium heat until slightly thickened, stirring constantly, about 2 minutes.

Stir cheeses into soup. Cook over medium heat until smooth, stirring frequently. Season with salt, pepper and cilantro. Garnish with diced chunks of plum tomatoes. *Yield: 5 cups.*

POTATO SOUP

3 C. peeled, diced potatoes
½ C. chopped onion
1 C. potato water
3 T. butter
1 tsp. salt

¼ tsp. pepper
3 C. milk
1 C. Cheddar cheese, shredded
¼ C. finely sliced green onions
   (optional)

In a saucepan, cover potatoes and onion with water and bring to a boil. Cover and simmer about 20 minutes or until soft. Reserve 1 cup of potato water; drain remaining water.

Place potatoes, onion, potato water, butter, salt and pepper in food processor and blend until smooth. Return to saucepan; add milk and cheese. Heat, stirring occasionally, until cheese melts. Garnish with green onions, if desired. *Yield: 4 servings.*

CREAM OF BROCCOLI SOUP

¼ C. vegetable oil
1 medium onion, chopped
1 large potato, peeled and
  diced
½ C. chopped celery
1 garlic clove, minced

Dash Tabasco
1 bunch broccoli, chopped
5 C. chicken broth
2 C. milk or half and half
1 T. dried basil
Salt to taste

Heat oil in a large saucepan over medium-high heat; add onion and sauté until tender. Add potato, celery, garlic and Tabasco. Cook 10 minutes, stirring occasionally. Stir in broccoli, chicken broth, milk and basil. Cover and simmer 20 minutes. Puree in food processor, add salt to taste and reheat in saucepan. *Yield: 12-14 servings.*

OKRA AND TOMATO GUMBO

¼ C. butter
1 C. chopped onion
1 clove garlic, chopped
1 pt. okra, sliced crosswise
1 qt. fresh tomatoes, cleaned
  and quartered

1 green pepper, seeded and
  chopped
1 bay leaf, crushed
2 T. parsley
2 tsp. salt

Melt butter in large pan over medium heat. Lightly sauté onion, garlic and okra in butter; add tomatoes, green pepper, bay leaf, parsley and salt. Simmer, covered, for 25 minutes. Serve over steamed rice, boiled potatoes or toast. *Yield: 4 servings.*

SAVANNAH GUMBO

2 T. oil
2 T. flour
1 C. onions, chopped
⅓ C. green onions, sliced
⅓ C. chopped green bell
   pepper
¼ C. chopped celery
2 garlic cloves, minced
3 C. chicken broth
1½ C. tomato juice
1 tsp. salt

¼ tsp. thyme leaves, crushed
½ tsp. cayenne pepper
2 bay leaves
1 (28 oz.) can tomatoes,
   undrained and cut up
1 (10 oz.) pkg. frozen cut okra
1½ lbs. medium shrimp,
   shelled and deveined
2 C. cooked chicken, cubed
4 C. hot cooked white rice

In a large skillet, combine oil and flour. Cook over medium heat 25-35 minutes until a dark reddish brown roux is formed. Stir frequently the first 15 minutes and constantly for the remainder of cooking time. Remove from heat; stir in onions, green onions, green pepper, celery and garlic until roux stops browning. Return to heat and cook on low until vegetables are tender.

Transfer to Dutch oven. Add chicken broth and tomato juice, stirring constantly. Add salt, thyme, cayenne pepper, bay leaves, tomatoes and okra. Bring to a boil. Reduce heat, cover and simmer 1 hour, stirring occasionally.

Remove bay leaves, then stir in shrimp and chicken. Simmer uncovered 3-5 minutes, until shrimp are light pink. To serve, place ½ cup rice in bowl and spoon about 1½ cups gumbo on top. *Yield: 8 servings.*

CREAMED TOMATO BISQUE

1 stick butter
2 C. chopped celery
1 C. chopped onion
½ C. chopped carrots
⅓ C. all-purpose flour
2 (1 lb. 12 oz.) cans whole
   tomatoes, drained and
   chopped
2 tsp. sugar

1 tsp. basil
1 tsp. marjoram
1 bay leaf
4 C. chicken broth
2 C. whipping cream
½ tsp. paprika
½ tsp. curry powder
¼ tsp. white pepper
Salt to taste

Melt butter in large saucepan. Sauté celery, onion and carrots until tender. Stir in flour. Cook 2 minutes, stirring constantly. Add next six ingredients; cover and simmer 30 minutes, stirring occasionally.

Discard bay leaf. Puree ⅓ of mixture at a time in blender. Return to saucepan and add whipping cream, paprika, curry powder and white pepper; stir to blend. Add salt to taste. Serve hot or cold. *Yield: 8 servings.*

VEGETABLE BEEF SOUP

1 large onion, coarsely
   chopped
2 stalks celery, sliced
3 large potatoes, cut into
   chunks
2 carrots, sliced thin
1 C. frozen butter beans
1 C. frozen corn

2 garlic cloves, minced
3 C. beef broth
2 (26 oz.) cans whole
   tomatoes
½ tsp. hot sauce
½ lb. sirloin, cut into chunks
Salt and pepper to taste

Place first seven ingredients in Dutch oven. Add broth, tomatoes and hot sauce; bring to a boil, reduce heat and simmer for 30 minutes. Add sirloin, salt and pepper; cook another 30 minutes until meat is tender. Serve warm. *Yield: 4 servings.*

STEAK SOUP AU ROUX

3 C. water
2 small onions, chopped
3 stalks celery, chopped
2 carrots, sliced
1 (14½ oz.) can tomatoes
½ tsp. pepper
1 (10 oz.) pkg. frozen mixed
 vegetables

1 lb. finely diced chuck roast,
 browned and drained
3 beef bouillon cubes
½ C. butter, melted
½ C. flour

Put all ingredients except butter and flour in a slow cooker. Cover and cook on low 8-10 hours; one hour before serving, turn heat to high. Just before serving, make a roux of butter and flour; cook, stirring, until smooth. Add roux to crock pot and stir until thickened. *Yield: 4 servings.*

BEEF TENDERLOIN SANDWICHES

½ C. boursin spread (p.10)
6 Kaiser rolls (others may be
 substituted)
½ lb. beef tenderloin, baked
 medium-rare and sliced thin

6 leaves green leaf lettuce
2 medium tomatoes, sliced
 thin

Make boursin spread according to recipe directions. Split rolls in half and spread inside of each half with boursin. Add slices of tenderloin, fresh lettuce leaves and sliced tomatoes. *Yield: 6 sandwiches.*

GRILLED STEAK SANDWICH WITH SALSA SPREAD

½ C. mayonnaise
¼ C. salsa, drained
¼ C. green onions, sliced thin
1 tsp. cilantro
1½ lbs. flank steaks

1 tsp. cracked black pepper
6 (¾" thick) slices sourdough
   or Italian bread
3 T. butter, melted
2 C. shredded iceberg lettuce

Combine mayonnaise, salsa, green onions and cilantro, mixing thoroughly; set aside. Coat both sides of steak with pepper; grill to desired doneness, turning once. Thinly slice steak across the grain.

Brush both sides of bread with melted butter and grill until brown.

For each serving: Spread one side of bread slice with 3 tablespoons salsa spread. Place on a plate, top with ⅓ cup lettuce and 4 oz. steak. Serve open faced. *Yield: 6 servings.*

Mexican Beef Pitas

1 lb. beef sirloin
⅓ C. olive oil
¼ C. lime juice
1 tsp. chili powder
1 tsp. red pepper flakes
1 large red onion, julienned
1 green bell pepper, julienned
1 red bell pepper, julienned

2 oz. hot green chili peppers, chopped
1 tsp. salt
6 pita breads, halved and warmed
1 C. alfalfa sprouts
1½ C. Monterey Jack cheese, shredded

Cut sirloin into ⅛" thick strips; set aside. Make a marinade by combining olive oil, lime juice, chili powder and red pepper flakes in a bowl; mix thoroughly.

Place beef in a heavy-duty plastic bag; place onion, green and red bell peppers and chili peppers in a separate bag. Add ⅓ cup marinade to beef; mix to coat thoroughly. Add remaining marinade to vegetables and mix to coat thoroughly. Close bags securely; refrigerate 20 minutes to 4 hours. Strain excess marinade from beef; discard marinade.

For each serving: Stir-fry vegetable mixture in hot skillet over medium-high heat 2 minutes (no additional oil should be needed). Add beef; continue to stir-fry 1-1½ minutes or until beef is no longer pink. Season lightly with salt.

For each serving: Open two pita bread halves; portion 2-3 tablespoons alfalfa sprouts and ¼ cup cheese into each. Fill each half with ½ cup of beef/vegetable mixture; serve immediately.
Yield: 6 servings.

PIMIENTO CHEESE SPREAD

1 T. all-purpose flour
2 T. sugar
1 T. vinegar
1 tsp. dry mustard
1 egg, beaten
1 T. butter or margarine

1 lb. pasteurized American
   cheese, shredded
1 (3 oz.) jar pimientos,
   chopped
2 T. mayonnaise
Salt and pepper to taste

Combine first six ingredients in a small saucepan; cook over low heat until thickened, stirring constantly. Remove from heat; pour over cheese and mash to blend ingredients. Add pimientos, mayonnaise, salt and pepper; mix well. Store in refrigerator until ready for use. *Yield: About 2½ cups.*

TURKEY-STUFFED PITA BREAD

6 pita bread rounds, cut in half
¼ lb. deli turkey breast, thin
   sliced (18-20 slices)
2 large tomatoes, sliced

1½ C. shredded iceberg
   lettuce
6 T. alfalfa sprouts
6 T. Italian dressing

For each sandwich: Open one pita bread half, placing 3 slices turkey breast, 2 slices tomato, ¼ cup lettuce and 1 tablespoon alfalfa sprouts in each half. Drizzle 1 tablespoon Italian dressing over contents of pita bread. Wrap in plastic wrap for overnight storage, or serve immediately. *Yield: 6 sandwiches.*

Vegetarian Mushroom and Avocado Sandwiches

3 large Portabello mushrooms	¼ C. light mayonnaise
2 T. butter or margarine	¾ C. alfalfa sprouts
2 avocados	1 large tomato, sliced thin
12 slices whole wheat or	1 red onion, sliced thin
rye bread	

Cut Portabello mushrooms into ¼" slices. In a medium saucepan, melt butter and sauté mushrooms for 3-4 minutes, until they just begin to become tender. Peel avocados, remove pits and slice thin, approximately 6-8 slices per avocado.

Spread bread slices with mayonnaise. Layer sandwiches by placing 1-2 mushroom slices on a piece of bread, followed by 2 avocado slices, 2 tablespoons alfalfa sprouts and 1 slice tomato. Top with a few red onion rings and place a second piece of bread on top to complete the sandwich. Cut in half diagonally to serve.
Yield: 6 servings.

Tomato Tea Sandwiches

12 thin slices white bread	Salt and pepper to taste
12 thin slices rye bread	¼ C. mayonnaise
4 ripe Roma tomatoes	

Cut bread slices into circles (two circles per slice). Cut tomatoes thin; sprinkle with salt and pepper. Spread bread with mayonnaise. Assemble sandwiches using 1 white slice and 1 rye slice per sandwich. *Yield: 24 small sandwiches.*

SOURDOUGH BREAD SANDWICH FOR A CROWD

1 round (8"-10" diameter) loaf
   sourdough bread
¼ C. salad mustard
¼ C. mayonnaise
½ lb. American cheese, sliced
½ lb. hard salami, sliced
½ lb. Mozzarella cheese,
   sliced

½ lb. deli ham, sliced
1 C. shredded lettuce
3 large tomatoes, sliced thin
1 (8 oz.) jar kosher dill pickles,
   sliced thin
⅓ C. light Italian dressing
½ tsp. celery salt
Pepper to taste

Slice bread loaf in half crosswise, spreading mustard and mayonnaise on each side of bread. Set upper half of loaf aside; layer American cheese, salami, Mozzarella and ham on bottom half of bread loaf. Top with shredded lettuce, sliced tomatoes and pickles. Drizzle Italian dressing over all. Sprinkle with the celery salt and pepper.

Place upper half of loaf on top of sandwich layers. Wrap entire loaf firmly in plastic wrap and refrigerate for several hours or until ready to serve.

To serve, cut pie-shaped wedges to desired thickness. Serve with chips and fresh fruit. *Yield: 12-14 servings.*

Note: A 36" loaf French bread may be substituted for the round sourdough loaf. Other meats and cheese may also be substituted if desired.

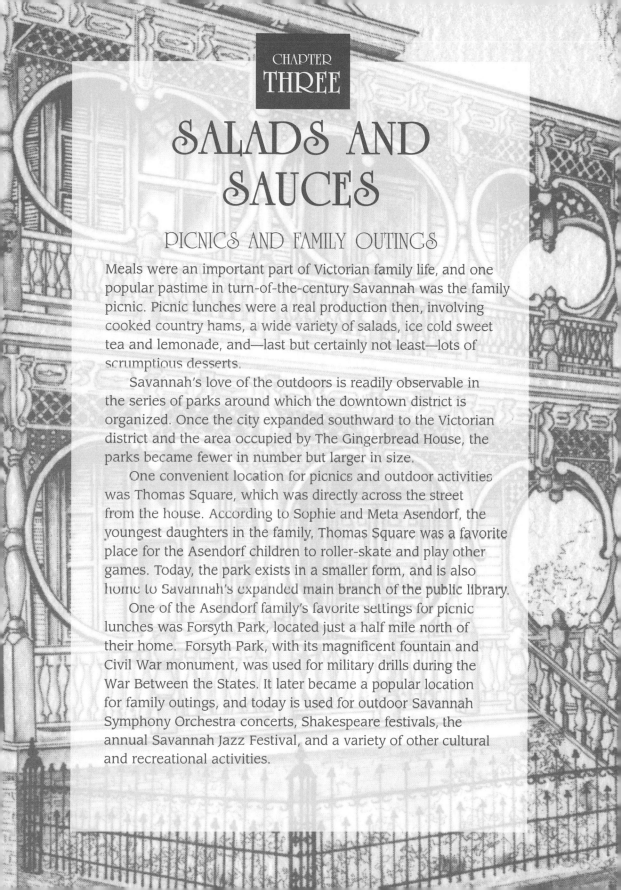

SALADS AND SAUCES

PICNICS AND FAMILY OUTINGS

Meals were an important part of Victorian family life, and one popular pastime in turn-of-the-century Savannah was the family picnic. Picnic lunches were a real production then, involving cooked country hams, a wide variety of salads, ice cold sweet tea and lemonade, and—last but certainly not least—lots of scrumptious desserts.

Savannah's love of the outdoors is readily observable in the series of parks around which the downtown district is organized. Once the city expanded southward to the Victorian district and the area occupied by The Gingerbread House, the parks became fewer in number but larger in size.

One convenient location for picnics and outdoor activities was Thomas Square, which was directly across the street from the house. According to Sophie and Meta Asendorf, the youngest daughters in the family, Thomas Square was a favorite place for the Asendorf children to roller-skate and play other games. Today, the park exists in a smaller form, and is also home to Savannah's expanded main branch of the public library.

One of the Asendorf family's favorite settings for picnic lunches was Forsyth Park, located just a half mile north of their home. Forsyth Park, with its magnificent fountain and Civil War monument, was used for military drills during the War Between the States. It later became a popular location for family outings, and today is used for outdoor Savannah Symphony Orchestra concerts, Shakespeare festivals, the annual Savannah Jazz Festival, and a variety of other cultural and recreational activities.

MENU

SOUTHERN-STYLE PICNIC

Sesame Apple Salad

Chilled Broccoli Salad

Bowtie Pasta with
Marinated Tomatoes and
Buffalo Mozzarella

Beef Tenderloin Sandwiches

Turkey-Stuffed Pita Bread

Apple, Oat
and Sesame Cookies

Sweet Clove Tea

This menu provides a nice balance of flavors,
textures, and colors. It also travels well,
so feel free to pack your picnic basket and
head to the park!

SESAME APPLE SALAD

1 C. unpeeled, chopped
   red apple
1 C. seedless green grape
   halves
1 C. sliced celery

⅓ C. orange-flavored low-fat
   yogurt
4 lettuce leaves
2 tsp. sesame seeds, toasted

Combine apple, grapes, celery and yogurt; toss gently. Spoon over lettuce leaves; sprinkle with sesame seeds. Serve immediately. *Yield: 4 servings.*

FRUIT SALAD WITH CREAM DRESSING

1½ tsp. grated orange rind
½ tsp. grated lemon rind
1½ T. orange juice
1 T. lemon juice
2 T. sugar
1 egg yolk, beaten
1½ tsp. butter or margarine

½ C. whipping cream
2 large red apples, cored and
   cubed
2 pears, cored and cubed
1 lb. seedless green grapes,
   halved

Combine first seven ingredients in top of a double boiler. Place over boiling water; cook, stirring constantly, 10-12 minutes or until thickened. Remove from boiling water; cool.

Beat whipping cream until soft peaks form; fold into cooled dressing mixture. Cover and chill up to 3 hours. To serve, combine apples, pears and grapes; toss gently with dressing and serve immediately. *Yield: 6-8 servings.*

WALNUT, PEAR AND BLEU CHEESE SALAD

1 head romaine lettuce (or a variety of mixed greens)
½ C. walnuts, coarsely chopped
1 firm pear, diced
½ C. bleu cheese, crumbled

5 T. salad oil
2 T. tarragon vinegar
½ tsp. dry mustard
Seasoned salt to taste
Fresh ground black pepper

Tear lettuce into bite-sized pieces and place in a salad bowl. Sprinkle with walnuts, diced pear and bleu cheese.

To make dressing, whisk together oil, vinegar, dry mustard and seasoned salt. Toss salad with dressing just before serving. Top with a generous grinding of fresh black pepper. *Yield: 4-6 servings.*

WATERGATE SALAD

1 large can crushed pineapple, drained
¼ C. maraschino cherries, coarsely chopped
½ C. pecans, chopped
1 C. miniature marshmallows

1 large pkg. pistachio instant pudding
1 (9 oz.) pkg. frozen whipped topping, thawed in refrigerator

Mix together all ingredients except whipped topping. Fold in whipped topping; refrigerate until ready to serve. *Yield: 6 servings.*

Mandarin Orange and Black Walnut Salad

1 head red leaf lettuce
1 head green leaf lettuce
½ C. Raspberry Vinaigrette
   Dressing (p. 60)
1 C. black walnuts, coarsely
   chopped

1 can mandarin oranges,
   drained
1 medium red onion, thinly
   sliced into rings

Tear red and green leaf lettuce into bite-sized pieces. Toss lettuce with vinaigrette dressing to coat. Place lettuce on salad plates. Arrange walnuts, mandarin oranges and onion on top. Serve immediately. *Yield: 6-8 servings.*

Marinated Vegetable Salad

1 can French cut green beans
1 can tiny green peas
1 (3 oz.) jar chopped pimiento
1 bell pepper, cut in thin strips
2 stalks celery, sliced
3 small white onions,
   sliced into rings

1 C. sugar
¾ C. white vinegar
½ C. salad oil
1 tsp. salt

Drain beans, peas and pimiento. Mix together with bell pepper, celery and onions. Make a marinade by mixing sugar, vinegar, salad oil and salt; pour over vegetables and refrigerate overnight. Drain before serving. *Yield: 6-8 servings.*

Note: Can substitute 1 can of corn niblets for peas. Mixture keeps for 1 week.

CHILLED BROCCOLI SALAD

1 bunch broccoli	1 red onion, chopped
½ head cauliflower	1 C. mayonnaise
10 slices bacon, fried and crumbled	½ C. sugar
	¼ C. wine vinegar
1 C. shredded Cheddar cheese	3 shakes seasoned salt

Cut broccoli and cauliflower into bite-sized pieces; do not cook. Toss broccoli, cauliflower, bacon, cheese and red onion together to mix.

Blend mayonnaise, sugar, vinegar and seasoned salt to make dressing. Stir into broccoli mixture; refrigerate until ready to serve. Will keep overnight. *Yield: 4-6 servings.*

MARINATED VIDALIA ONION SALAD

5 large Vidalia sweet onions	½ C. mayonnaise
½ C. cider vinegar	¼ tsp. celery salt
2 C. water	2 bunches green leaf lettuce
1 C. sugar	1 pkg. butter crackers

Cut onions into very thin slices. Mix together vinegar, water and sugar; soak onions in this mixture for 24 hours in the refrigerator.

Drain onions thoroughly in colander, then pat dry with paper towels. Just before serving, mix onions with mayonnaise and celery salt. Serve on a bed of lettuce with butter crackers. *Yield: 8-10 servings.*

TOMATOES AND MOZZARELLA WITH ARTICHOKE VINAIGRETTE

2 lbs. ripe plum tomatoes, thinly sliced
1 lb. Mozzarella cheese, sliced
2 (6 oz.) jars marinated artichoke hearts
1 tsp. salt

1 red onion, sliced thin
10 pitted black olives, quartered
2 T. capers, drained
1 tsp. dried basil leaves

Using a large platter, alternate layers of half the tomatoes and cheese, followed by the remaining tomatoes and cheese. Drain artichokes, reserving marinade, and place in the center of the platter; sprinkle with salt. Scatter onion slices, olives, capers and basil leaves over top of entire platter. Drizzle reserved marinade over all. Let stand at room temperature at least 1 hour before serving. *Yield: 8 servings.*

HEARTS OF PALM SALAD

1 C. olive oil
½ C. white vinegar
½ C. finely chopped celery
¼ C. finely chopped red pepper
¼ C. finely chopped onion

2 cloves garlic, pressed
1 (16 oz.) can hearts of palm, drained and cut into ½" pieces
6 C. romaine lettuce, torn

Combine first six ingredients to make dressing; chill at least 8 hours. To serve, arrange hearts of palm on top of lettuce on individual serving plates; top with dressing. *Yield: 6 servings.*

DIXIE COLE SLAW

1 medium head cabbage,
   shredded
3 large carrots, grated
1 C. mayonnaise

¼ C. sugar
2 T. white vinegar
1 tsp. celery salt

Toss cabbage and carrots together; set aside. In a small bowl, make a dressing by mixing mayonnaise, sugar, vinegar and celery salt until smooth.

Toss cabbage and carrots with dressing. Can refrigerate 3-5 hours before serving. *Yield: 8 servings.*

CREAMY POTATO SALAD

6 C. potatoes, boiled, cooled
   and diced
3 hard-boiled eggs, cooled,
   peeled and chopped
¼ C. sweet pickle relish
1 medium onion, finely
   chopped

1 tsp. salt
2 T. chopped chives
½ tsp. dry mustard
1¼ C. mayonnaise
Cherry tomatoes and fresh
   parsley for garnish

Gently mix potatoes, eggs, pickle relish, onion and salt together; fold in chives and dry mustard; adjust seasonings to taste. Toss gently with just enough mayonnaise to bind mixture together. Refrigerate for several hours or overnight. Serve garnished with cherry tomatoes and fresh parsley, if desired. *Yield: 8 servings.*

CURRIED CHICKEN SALAD

6 boneless chicken breast
  halves
1 medium onion, finely
  chopped
2 ribs celery, finely chopped

⅓ C. sweet pickle relish
1 T. lemon juice
½ C. mayonnaise
1 tsp. curry powder
Salt and pepper to taste

Boil chicken in water until cooked, about 20-25 minutes; drain and skin chicken. Chop chicken in food processor or by hand (finely chopped for sandwich filling; coarsely chopped or diced for salad). Add remaining ingredients and stir to blend. Serve on a bed of lettuce, stuffed in beefsteak tomatoes, or as sandwich filling. *Yield: 4 servings.*

CRAB SALAD

1 (1 lb.) can lump crab meat,
  drained
2 to 3 T. mayonnaise or
  cream cheese

¼ C. finely chopped celery
½ tsp. seasoned salt
1 T. chopped chives
1 tsp. parsley flakes

Mix all ingredients together, tossing lightly to blend. Serve with assorted breads and crackers or on lettuce leaves. Mixture may also be served stuffed in tomatoes, avocados or artichokes. *Yield: 4 servings.*

SHRIMP SALAD

1 lb. shrimp, coarsely chopped
½ C. chopped celery
3 T. finely chopped onion
2 hard-boiled eggs, peeled and chopped
1 T. lemon juice
2 T. chives
Salt and pepper to taste
½ C. mayonnaise

Toss shrimp, celery, onion and eggs together to blend; fold in lemon juice and chives; add salt and pepper to taste. Add just enough mayonnaise to bind mixture together. Chill until ready to serve, 3-4 hours or overnight.

May be served on a bed of lettuce, open-faced on slices of French bread, or with rye bread as sandwiches. *Yield: 4 servings.*

TACO SALAD

1 lb. ground chuck
1 clove garlic, minced
1 small onion, chopped
1 green pepper, seeded and
   chopped
1 (16 oz.) can tomatoes,
   drained and chopped
1 T. chili powder
1 tsp. cumin
½ tsp. oregano
Salt and pepper to taste

1 head iceberg lettuce,
   shredded
6 oz. tortilla chips, crumbled
4 oz. sharp Cheddar cheese,
   grated
2 fresh tomatoes, coarsely
   chopped
4-5 scallions, chopped
Toppings: Sour cream, bottled
   taco sauce, guacamole
   (optional)

Sauté beef, garlic, onion and green pepper in a skillet until meat is browned. Drain grease. Stir in canned tomatoes, chili powder, cumin, oregano, salt and pepper. Cook 15 minutes, uncovered, stirring occasionally.

Place lettuce in a large salad bowl and toss with tortilla chips, cheese, tomatoes and scallions. Spoon hot beef mixture on top and toss gently.

Serve immediately. Pass sour cream, taco sauce and guacamole on the side. *Yield: 4 servings.*

Seafood Cocktail Sauce

1 C. catsup
1/3 C. horseradish
1/4 C. lemon juice

1/4 tsp. grated onion
1 tsp. Worcestershire sauce

Mix all together; chill until ready for use. Serve, garnished with lemon slices, with shrimp cocktail or crab. *Yield: 1 1/3 cups.*

Honey Mustard Sauce

1/4 C. vegetable oil
1/4 C. spicy brown or Dijon
   mustard
3-4 T. honey

2 T. dry sherry or white wine
1 T. red wine vinegar
1 tsp. grated lemon peel

Mix all ingredients until well blended. Makes a good sauce to serve with chicken nuggets; may also be used as a dressing for salad. *Yield: Approximately 2/3 cup.*

SPECIAL BARBECUE SAUCE

1 qt. apple cider vinegar
1 pt. mustard
9 C. catsup
3 T. salt
¼ C. coarse pepper

1 small bottle (12 oz.)
   Worcestershire sauce
1 stick butter
1 T. sugar
Juice of 1 lemon

Mix all ingredients together in large saucepan and simmer 5-6 hours. Recipe makes enough to use throughout the summer barbecue season. *Yield: Approximately 1 gallon.*

BARBECUE CHILI BUTTER

2 sticks unsalted butter, room
   temperature
2 T. lemon juice
2 T. mixed chopped herbs
   (parsley, rosemary, thyme,
   chives, basil, etc.)
2 anchovies, finely chopped
   (optional)

1 T. chopped shallot
¼ C. smoked barbecue sauce
2 jalapeno chilies, finely
   chopped
Pinch of salt and ground
   black pepper

Place all ingredients in a food processor and blend for 1-2 minutes, until the butter is smooth and shiny. Roll butter in waxed paper and refrigerate. May also be frozen for later use.

Makes a delicious topping for steak, grilled chicken or pork tenderloin. *Yield: 1¼ cups.*

Raspberry Vinaigrette Dressing

2 tsp. Dijon mustard
Pinch salt
Pinch fresh ground
 pepper

2-4 T. raspberry wine vinegar
 (or white wine vinegar, if
 preferred)
1-1½ C. olive oil

In a small bowl, mix together mustard, salt, pepper and wine vinegar. Add olive oil, drizzling slowly and mixing with a wire whisk until all is incorporated. Taste and adjust seasonings if desired. Refrigerate until ready for use. *Yield: 1½ cups.*

Béarnaise Sauce

½ C. dry white wine
¼ C. tarragon vinegar
2 tsp. dried tarragon
½ tsp. freshly ground pepper

8 egg yolks, room temperature
¼ C. lemon juice
½ tsp. hot sauce
2 C. butter, melted

In a small saucepan, combine white wine, vinegar, dried tarragon and pepper. Bring to a boil and cook until reduced to ¼ cup.

Combine egg yolks, lemon juice and hot sauce in food processor and mix for 10-15 seconds. With machine running, add melted butter and wine mixture.

May be used as topping for tenderloin, as a sandwich spread or for topping vegetables. *Yield: Approximately 2¼ cups.*

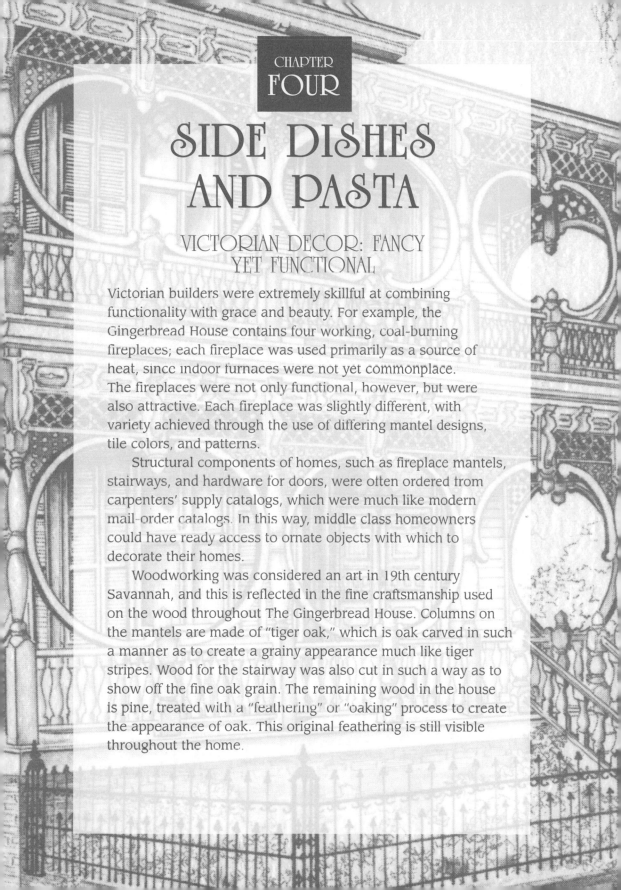

SIDE DISHES AND PASTA

VICTORIAN DECOR: FANCY YET FUNCTIONAL

Victorian builders were extremely skillful at combining functionality with grace and beauty. For example, the Gingerbread House contains four working, coal-burning fireplaces; each fireplace was used primarily as a source of heat, since indoor furnaces were not yet commonplace. The fireplaces were not only functional, however, but were also attractive. Each fireplace was slightly different, with variety achieved through the use of differing mantel designs, tile colors, and patterns.

Structural components of homes, such as fireplace mantels, stairways, and hardware for doors, were often ordered from carpenters' supply catalogs, which were much like modern mail-order catalogs. In this way, middle class homeowners could have ready access to ornate objects with which to decorate their homes.

Woodworking was considered an art in 19th century Savannah, and this is reflected in the fine craftsmanship used on the wood throughout The Gingerbread House. Columns on the mantels are made of "tiger oak," which is oak carved in such a manner as to create a grainy appearance much like tiger stripes. Wood for the stairway was also cut in such a way as to show off the fine oak grain. The remaining wood in the house is pine, treated with a "feathering" or "oaking" process to create the appearance of oak. This original feathering is still visible throughout the home.

MENU

SPECIAL OCCASION

SUPER BOWL PARTY

Mexican Layered Dip with
Tortilla Chips

Cheddar Cheese Pecan Log

Sour Cream Spinach Dip with
Brittle Bread

Dijon Crab Dip

Shrimp Steamed in Beer

Seafood Cocktail Sauce

Sausage Meatballs in Barbecue Sauce

Sourdough Bread Sandwich For a Crowd

Oven-Roasted Salted Pecans

Assorted Beverages

This is a great menu for the party host who's also
an avid sports fan. All the menu items can be prepared
ahead and placed on a buffet table for self-service.
Keep plenty of chips and crackers on hand to
accompany the dips.

ASPARAGUS CASSEROLE

2 eggs, lightly beaten
1 C. milk
1 C. coarsely crushed crackers
1 (10½ oz.) can green cut
  asparagus spears, undrained

1 C. shredded sharp Cheddar
  cheese
⅛ tsp. hot sauce
Paprika

Combine eggs and milk in a medium mixing bowl, beating well. Stir in crackers, asparagus, cheese and hot sauce. Pour mixture into a greased 1-quart casserole. Sprinkle with paprika. Bake at 375° for 45 minutes or until puffed and browned. Serve immediately.
Yield: 4 servings.

BROCCOLI CASSEROLE

1 (10 oz.) pkg. frozen chopped
  broccoli
¾ C. grated cheese
1 small onion, grated
¼ pkg. herb-seasoned stuffing

1 can cream of mushroom
  soup
½ C. mayonnaise
½ C. melted butter
2 eggs, beaten

Thaw broccoli, but do not cook. Mix all ingredients together and place in greased casserole. Bake at 350° until brown or mixture is set, about 40-45 minutes. *Yield: 4 servings.*

Note: Spinach or asparagus can be substituted in this recipe.

Honey Buttered Carrots

2 lbs. carrots, cut in 2"
  julienne strips
1 tsp. salt
½ C. honey

2 T. butter
2 T. brown sugar
1 tsp. nutmeg

Cook carrots in boiling water for 2 minutes; drain and rinse with cold water. Return to pan and add salt, honey, butter, brown sugar and nutmeg. Cover and cook an additional 3-5 minutes until carrots are crisp-tender but not overcooked. *Yield: 6 servings.*

Fried Squash

1½ C. cornmeal
1 tsp. salt

½ C. vegetable oil
1 lb. yellow squash

In a plastic or paper bag, mix cornmeal and salt together. Set aside. Heat vegetable oil in a medium skillet. Meanwhile, clean squash and cut crosswise into ¼" slices. Coat squash slices with cornmeal mixture by shaking in bag or covered container.

Sauté squash in a single layer over medium-high heat until squash begins to brown on the bottom. Turn each piece, continuing to cook until squash is crisp-tender and lightly browned. Remove from skillet and drain on paper towel. Serve hot. *Yield: 4 servings.*

Squash Casserole

2 lbs. yellow squash
1 large onion, chopped
1 stick butter
1 C. sour cream
1 can cream of mushroom
  soup
Salt and pepper to taste
1 small bag herb stuffing

Boil squash until tender; drain and mash. Sauté onion in butter. Mix squash, onion, sour cream, soup, salt, pepper and half of the stuffing mix. Pour into casserole. Sprinkle remaining stuffing mix over top and bake at 300° for 1 hour. *Yield: 6 servings.*

Baked Acorn Squash

4 medium acorn squash
1½ tsp. salt
½ tsp. pepper
½ C. butter or margarine
¼ C. tawny port
¼ C. maple syrup
1 (14 oz.) jar cranberry-orange
  relish

Cut squash in half lengthwise. Place squash halves in a shallow baking pan. Rub a small amount of salt and pepper into the flesh of each squash. In center cavity of each squash, place 1 tablespoon butter or margarine and 1½ teaspoons each tawny port and maple syrup. Cover squash loosely with foil and pour a little hot water into baking pan. Bake 30-40 minutes at 375° or until tender.

Combine cooking liquid from center of squash halves with cranberry-orange relish. Heat and stir to mix well. Fill each squash half with 2 tablespoons cranberry-orange relish and serve the remaining relish alongside. *Yield: 6-8 servings.*

RATATOUILLE CASSEROLE

2 large onions, sliced
2 large cloves garlic, minced
1 medium eggplant, peeled and cubed
6 medium zucchini, thickly sliced
2 bell peppers, seeded and cut into chunks
4 large tomatoes, coarsely chopped
2 tsp. salt
1 tsp. basil
½ C. parsley, minced
¼ C. olive oil
2 C. Mozzarella cheese, shredded

Layer onions, garlic, eggplant, zucchini, bell peppers and tomatoes in a greased 6-quart casserole. Sprinkle a little salt, basil and parsley between each layer. Drizzle olive oil over top layer. Reserve cheese for later.

Cover and bake at 350° for 3 hours, basting the top occasionally with liquid. If casserole becomes soupy, uncover during the last hour of cooking to let juices cook down. Sprinkle Mozzarella on top during the last 30 minutes of cooking, leaving uncovered.

Mix gently after removing from oven. Add salt to taste. May be served hot or cold. *Yield: 15 servings.*

GREEN BEANS WITH MUSHROOMS AND PARMESAN

2 lbs. whole green beans or
  2 (10 oz.) pkgs. frozen
  whole green beans
Salt to taste
2 C. sliced mushrooms
½ C. chopped onion
1 clove garlic, crushed

2 T. butter or margarine
¾ C. sour cream
1 tsp. salt
¼ tsp. pepper
½ C. fresh bread crumbs
¼ C. grated Parmesan cheese

Snip both ends from whole green beans and cook in boiling salted water until just tender, about 3-5 minutes. (Or, cook frozen whole green beans according to package directions, but for only half the cooking time.) Drain well.

In a skillet, sauté sliced mushrooms, onion and garlic in butter or margarine until tender. Stir into drained beans, together with sour cream, salt and pepper.

Turn into a 2-quart casserole and sprinkle top with a mixture of fresh bread crumbs and Parmesan cheese. Bake at 350° for 20-25 minutes, or until top is bubbly and golden. *Yield: 6-8 servings.*

Italian Eggplant

1 medium eggplant
1 egg, beaten
2 T. water
½ tsp. salt
⅓ C. vegetable oil

¼ lb. Mozzarella cheese,
  sliced
¼ C. minced onion
¼ tsp. oregano
1 C. tomato sauce

Peel and cut eggplant into ¼" crosswise slices. Combine egg, water and salt. Dip each slice of eggplant in egg mixture.

In a skillet, heat oil; sauté eggplant slowly in oil until brown on both sides. Place eggplant slices in 2-quart casserole with a slice of cheese between and on top. Add onion and oregano to tomato sauce and heap around eggplant. Bake at 375° until cheese is melted and browned. *Yield: 4 servings.*

Baked Tomatoes Stuffed with Boursin

3 large ripe tomatoes
½ tsp. salt
¾ C. boursin spread
  (p.10)

Chopped fresh parsley
  (optional)

Preheat oven to 350°. Wash tomatoes and slice in half. Sprinkle each tomato half with salt. Spread 2 tablespoons boursin on top of each half. Place tomatoes on ungreased baking sheet; bake for 40 minutes or until center of tomato is tender when pierced with fork. Remove from oven; garnish with chopped fresh parsley, if desired, and serve immediately. *Yield: 6 servings.*

SPINACH-STUFFED TOMATOES

6 large ripe tomatoes
1 (10 oz.) pkg. frozen chopped
    spinach, thawed
3 T. olive oil
¾ C. chopped onion

½ C. Italian bread crumbs
½ tsp. salt
⅛ tsp. ground black pepper
6 T. Parmesan cheese

Preheat oven to 375°. Cut a ½" slice from the top of each tomato.
Scoop out pulp, chop and set aside. Place tomato shells upside down
to drain. Squeeze as much liquid from spinach as possible; set aside.

In a skillet, heat olive oil. Add onion, bread crumbs, salt, pepper,
reserved chopped tomato and spinach. Cook and stir until hot.

Spoon mixture into tomato shells, piling high. Sprinkle each tomato
with 1 tablespoon Parmesan cheese. Place in a greased 10" x 6" x 2"
baking pan. Bake, uncovered, until tomatoes are soft, about
30 minutes. *Yield: 6 servings.*

HERBED POTATOES

½ C. butter, melted
2 T. chopped fresh chives
2 T. chopped parsley
¼ tsp. paprika
1 tsp. salt

¼ tsp. pepper
4½ lbs. potatoes, unpeeled
 and cut into ¼" slices
½ C. grated Parmesan cheese

Combine first six ingredients in a large bowl; add potatoes, tossing to coat. Place in a baking dish. Cover; bake at 425° for 1 hour, stirring every 15 minutes. Top with grated cheese. *Yield: 12 servings.*

TWICE-BAKED POTATOES

6 medium-large baking
 potatoes
2 T. butter, softened
1 C. sour cream
1 small onion, grated

1 tsp. salt
¼ tsp. cayenne pepper
1 C. deli ham, coarsely
 chopped
1 C. shredded Cheddar cheese

Bake potatoes at 400° for 1 hour or until done; while still warm, cut potatoes in half lengthwise and scoop out insides, leaving approximately ⅛" around the edge of each potato.

Mash potatoes, butter, sour cream, onion and seasonings until smooth; stir in ham. Place potato skins on baking sheet; fill with potato mixture and bake at 375° for 15-20 minutes or until hot. Sprinkle with cheese and return to oven to bake until cheese melts. *Yield: 5-6 servings.*

ONION ROASTED POTATOES

1 envelope onion soup mix
¼ C. vegetable oil
¼ C. butter, melted
¼ tsp. pepper
2 lbs. all-purpose red
    potatoes, cut in 1" cubes

¼ C. each chopped red and
    green bell pepper
Fresh chopped parsley for
    garnish

Preheat oven to 400°. In shallow baking pan, thoroughly blend soup mix, oil, butter and pepper. Add potatoes and stir to coat thoroughly. Bake, stirring occasionally, for 30 minutes; stir in chopped peppers and bake an additional 30 minutes or until potatoes are tender and golden brown.

Garnish with chopped parsley and serve immediately.
Yield: 8 servings.

GLAZED SWEET POTATOES

2 large sweet potatoes
¼ C. firmly packed light brown
   sugar
¼ C. pure cane syrup
2 T. dark molasses
1 T. dark corn syrup

Dash nutmeg
⅛ tsp. ground cloves
Dash ground allspice
⅛ tsp. ground cinnamon
¼ tsp. dry mustard
2 T. water

Preheat oven to 400°. Grease a 2-quart glass rectangular baking dish. Prepare sweet potatoes by washing, removing ends and cutting into 1" cubes. Set aside.

Combine next eight ingredients in a medium bowl. In another bowl, dissolve the dry mustard in the water, then add to the blended spice mixture.

Toss sweet potatoes in a large mixing bowl with the glaze to coat evenly. Pour into prepared dish and roast until fork tender, about 1 hour. Serve warm. *Yield: 10 servings.*

HAM AND VEGETABLE QUICHE

Pastry for 9" pie
½ C. chopped cauliflower
¼ C. chopped carrots
¼ C. chopped onions
¼ C. chopped green pepper

1 C. ham, coarsely chopped
1 C. shredded Cheddar cheese
1 C. milk
½ tsp. salt
3 eggs, beaten

Line a 9" quiche dish with pastry, trimming excess pastry around edges. Prick bottom and sides with a fork; bake at 425° for 5 minutes, then cool.

Cook next four ingredients in boiling water for 5 minutes or until tender; drain in colander. Mix in chopped ham and shredded cheese.

Add milk and salt to beaten eggs, then combine with ham/vegetable mixture. Pour into quiche pan and bake in preheated 350° oven for 30-40 minutes, or until knife inserted in center comes out clean. *Yield: 8 servings.*

SMOKY BAKED BEANS

3 slices uncooked bacon,
  chopped
2 T. diced onion
1 C. catsup
1 tsp. cider vinegar
1 T. molasses
¼ C. packed brown sugar

1 T. Worcestershire sauce
¼ tsp. liquid smoke
1 tsp. dry mustard
¼ tsp. black pepper
2 (16 oz.) cans pinto beans,
  drained and rinsed

Sauté bacon until brown; add onion to bacon and sauté until transparent. Add all other ingredients except beans and bring to a boil.

Reduce heat and simmer for 10 minutes. Add sauce to beans, then bake, uncovered, at 300° for 1 hour. *Yield: 6-8 servings.*

CASHEW RICE PILAF WITH BABY GREEN PEAS

⅓ C. chopped onion
¼ C. butter
1 C. uncooked rice
2 C. chicken broth

1 tsp. salt
⅓ C. frozen baby green peas
½ C. chopped cashews
¼ C. chopped parsley

Sauté onion in butter until soft. Stir in rice until coated. Add broth and salt. Cover and simmer 25-30 minutes until rice is tender and liquid is absorbed. Stir in peas, cashews and parsley. Serve immediately. *Yield: 6 servings.*

ALMOND RICE

¼ C. chopped almonds
3 T. butter, melted
3 C. cooked long-grain rice

⅓ C. minced parsley
⅛ tsp. curry powder

Sauté almonds in butter. Remove from heat; add remaining ingredients. *Yield: 4-6 servings.*

Fettuccine Alfredo

1 lb. fettuccine
6 T. butter
¾ C. heavy cream

1 egg yolk
6 T. grated Parmesan cheese
Salt and pepper to taste

Cook fettuccine according to the package directions until al dente, 6-8 minutes. Melt butter in a sauté pan and add the freshly cooked fettuccine; toss gently with two forks until pasta is well coated with butter.

Blend together heavy cream and egg yolk; add to fettuccine, sprinkle with grated Parmesan cheese, salt and pepper and blend well. Serve immediately. *Yield: 6 servings.*

Bowtie Pasta with Marinated Tomatoes and Buffalo Mozzarella

2 large ripe tomatoes
2 balls buffalo Mozzarella
   cheese
¼ C. olive oil
2 T. dry basil

2 cloves fresh garlic
1½ tsp. salt
2 tsp. cracked pepper
1 lb. bowtie or other small
   pasta

Dice tomatoes and cheese. Pour oil and basil over tomato mix; add pressed garlic, salt and pepper. Set aside.

Cook pasta until tender; drain and toss with tomato mixture. Cover and let set 5 minutes to warm tomatoes and melt cheese. *Yield: 4-6 servings.*

Note: Can substitute 2 cups diced regular Mozzarella, although texture and taste will differ somewhat.

VEGETABLE LASAGNA

1 ¼ C. Ricotta cheese
2 T. chopped fresh basil
1 tsp. oregano
¼ tsp. grated nutmeg
Salt and pepper to taste
Tabasco to taste
½ C. grated Mozzarella
  cheese
¼ C. grated Parmesan cheese
2 tsp. olive oil
¼ C. butter
1 large red onion, halved and
  thinly sliced

1 large zucchini, trimmed,
  halved lengthwise and thinly
  sliced
8 large mushrooms, thinly
  sliced
1 tsp. chopped garlic
Salt and pepper to taste
3 T. canned chicken broth
2 tsp. basil
2 T. chopped parsley
9 lasagna noodles

Preheat oven to 350°. Combine Ricotta cheese, basil, oregano and nutmeg; season with salt, pepper and Tabasco to taste. Set aside cheese mixture, Mozzarella and Parmesan.

Heat olive oil and butter in a large saucepan; add onion, zucchini, mushrooms and garlic. Sauté until onion is translucent and zucchini and mushrooms are tender. Add salt and pepper, chicken broth, basil and parsley. Cook on low for an additional 5 minutes.

Cook lasagna noodles according to package directions; cut in half crosswise. Layer half of lasagna in a 9" x 13" baking dish, followed by half of the vegetable mixture and Ricotta cheese. Sprinkle with Mozzarella and Parmesan, then repeat layers, ending with Mozzarella and Parmesan. Bake for 45 minutes, or until top is brown and bubbly. Remove from oven, let stand for 5 minutes, then cut and serve. *Yield: 4-6 servings.*

CLASSIC LASAGNA

3 lbs. bulk spicy sausage
4 medium onions, chopped
4 cloves garlic, minced
2 large cans Italian plum
  tomatoes (1 lb. 12 oz. each),
  drained and chopped
1 small can tomato paste
½ C. dry vermouth
1 tsp. basil
1 tsp. oregano

½ C. chopped parsley
Salt and pepper to taste
½ C. grated Parmesan cheese
¼ C. butter
1 lb. mushrooms, sliced
1 lb. Ricotta cheese
2 eggs, beaten
1 pkg. lasagna noodles
2 C. grated Mozzarella cheese

Preheat oven to 375°. Sauté sausage, onions and garlic in a large pan or Dutch oven. Drain well and return to pan. Add tomatoes, tomato paste, vermouth, basil, oregano, parsley, salt, pepper and Parmesan cheese. Bring to a boil, reduce heat and simmer for 30 minutes. Sauce will be very thick.

Melt butter and sauté mushrooms until soft. Stir mushrooms and butter into sauce. Combine Ricotta cheese and eggs separately.

Cook lasagna noodles according to package directions. Rinse well in cold water and drain.

In a large rectangular baking dish, spread a thin layer of sauce. Top with layer of noodles, followed by a layer of sauce, Ricotta cheese mixture and Mozzarella cheese. Keep repeating, ending with noodles, sauce and cheese.

Bake for 30 minutes. Let stand 5 minutes, then cut and serve.
Yield: 8-10 servings.

OLD-FASHIONED SPAGHETTI AND MEATBALLS

1 lb. bulk sausage
1 C. dry bread crumbs
3 cloves garlic, minced
1½ tsp. salt
1 tsp. oregano
1 tsp. pepper
2 eggs
⅓ C. olive oil
3 T. finely chopped parsley

1 (29 oz.) can tomato sauce
2 large ripe tomatoes, cut into
  chunks
2 T. Italian seasoning
1 green pepper, chopped
¼ C. chopped onion
1 T. butter
8 oz. spaghetti
3 T. grated Parmesan cheese

In a 2-quart bowl, mix together sausage, bread crumbs, garlic, salt, oregano, pepper, eggs, olive oil and parsley. Shape into medium size balls.

Place meatballs on a baking sheet and bake at 350° for 20 minutes or until browned. Drain excess fat.

Place tomato sauce and fresh tomato chunks in a large saucepan. Add Italian seasoning and stir to mix.

Sauté green pepper and onion in butter until onion is translucent and pepper is crisp-tender, then add to tomato sauce. Add meatballs, stir gently to mix, then simmer for 45 minutes.

Cook spaghetti according to package directions. Serve sauce and meatballs over spaghetti topped with Parmesan cheese.
Yield: 4 servings.

BOWTIE PASTA WITH GRILLED CHICKEN

8 oz. bowtie pasta
2 C. grilled, sautéed or baked chicken
1 clove garlic, minced
6 green onions, cut in thin slices (use tops)
2 T. olive oil
1 red bell pepper, cut in slivers
1 each zucchini and yellow squash, cut in matchsticks
1 (28 oz.) can chopped tomatoes, undrained
Splash white balsamic vinegar
1 handful fresh spinach
1 C. garbanzo beans (optional)
Grated Parmesan cheese for topping

Cook bowtie pasta according to package directions. While pasta is cooking, prepare the rest of the dish.

Cut chicken into ¼" x 2" strips, then set aside. Sauté garlic and green onions in a tiny amount of olive oil. Add bell pepper, zucchini and squash and sauté until tender but still crisp. Add tomatoes and cook until tomato juice bubbles. Add splash of vinegar, then add spinach greens, cover and allow to steam until wilted.

Place pasta on platter and top with sautéed vegetables. Lay grilled chicken slivers over vegetables; toss garbanzo beans on top and sprinkle with Parmesan cheese. *Yield: 6 servings.*

ROTINI WITH PEPPERS, PEPPERONI AND CHEESE

8 oz. tri-colored rotini pasta
1 C. chicken broth
2 cloves garlic, crushed
1½ oz. pepperoni, thinly sliced and cut into quarters
1 red bell pepper, seeded and cut into 1" squares
1 yellow bell pepper, seeded and cut into 1" squares
1 green bell pepper, seeded and cut into 1" squares
½ C. seeded, diced tomato
½ tsp. dried basil
½ tsp. dried oregano
¼ tsp. freshly ground black pepper
⅛ tsp. salt
2 oz. Mozzarella cheese, cut into ½" pieces
¼ C. fresh basil leaves, coarsely chopped (or, ⅛ C. dried basil leaves)

Cook pasta according to package directions. While pasta is cooking, prepare the rest of the dish.

In a large, nonstick skillet, bring ½ cup of the chicken broth to a boil. Add garlic and cook 1 minute longer. Add pepperoni and cook 1 minute, stirring to separate the slices. Add the bell peppers, tomato, remaining chicken broth, ½ teaspoon basil, oregano, pepper and salt. Adjust heat so the broth is simmering but not boiling and cook for 5-6 minutes, or until the bell peppers are tender. (When cooking the sauce, about half the broth will evaporate. If the mixture seems too dry, add a few tablespoons of reserved broth.)

Stir in cheese and cook until cheese is soft but not melted. Add ¼ cup basil, pour sauce over pasta and serve immediately.
Yield: 4-6 servings.

MANICOTTI

1 medium onion, chopped
2-4 cloves garlic, pressed
½ lb. Italian sausage
2 T. olive oil
2 (16 oz.) cans whole
  tomatoes, chopped
2 T. tomato paste
1 tsp. oregano
1 tsp. thyme
1 tsp. salt
2 T. chopped fresh parsley
2 bay leaves

½ tsp. pepper
1 (10 oz.) pkg. frozen chopped
  spinach
16 oz. Ricotta cheese
8 oz. freshly grated Parmesan
  cheese
1 T. fresh or 1 tsp. dried basil
1 (8 oz.) pkg. manicotti shells
1 T. olive oil
8 oz. Mozzarella cheese,
  grated

To make sauce, sauté onion, garlic and sausage in olive oil. Add tomatoes, tomato paste, oregano, thyme, salt, parsley, bay leaves and pepper; cook slowly until thick. Set aside, keeping warm.

For filling, cook spinach and drain well. Combine Ricotta, Parmesan, spinach and basil.

Cook pasta according to package directions, adding 1 tablespoon olive oil in the water. Drain and rinse with cold water.

To assemble, place a spoonful of sauce in casserole to line bottom. Fill shells and place in casserole in one layer. Cover with sauce and top with grated Mozzarella. Bake 45 minutes in a preheated 350° oven. *Yield: 6 servings.*

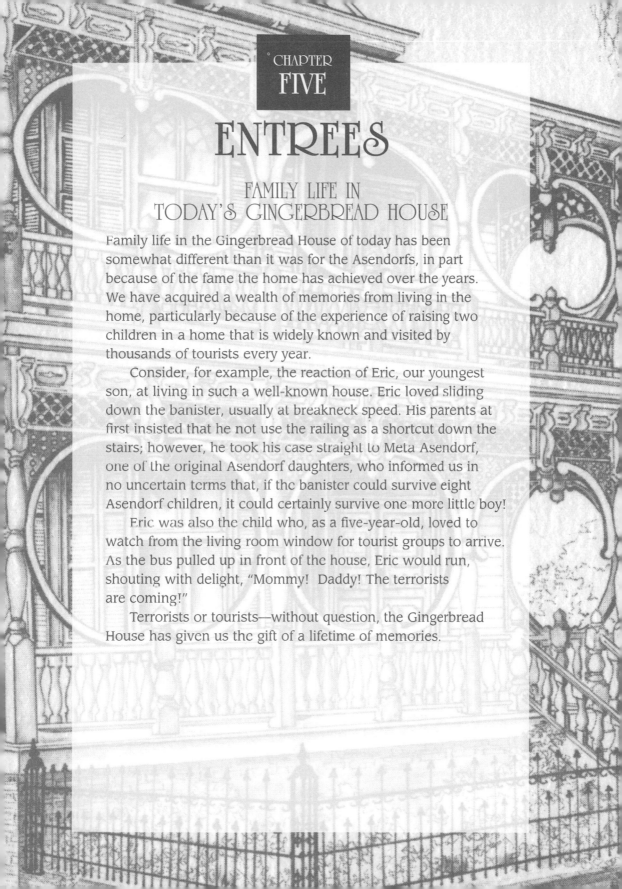

CHAPTER FIVE

ENTREES

FAMILY LIFE IN TODAY'S GINGERBREAD HOUSE

Family life in the Gingerbread House of today has been somewhat different than it was for the Asendorfs, in part because of the fame the home has achieved over the years. We have acquired a wealth of memories from living in the home, particularly because of the experience of raising two children in a home that is widely known and visited by thousands of tourists every year.

Consider, for example, the reaction of Eric, our youngest son, at living in such a well-known house. Eric loved sliding down the banister, usually at breakneck speed. His parents at first insisted that he not use the railing as a shortcut down the stairs; however, he took his case straight to Meta Asendorf, one of the original Asendorf daughters, who informed us in no uncertain terms that, if the banister could survive eight Asendorf children, it could certainly survive one more little boy!

Eric was also the child who, as a five-year-old, loved to watch from the living room window for tourist groups to arrive. As the bus pulled up in front of the house, Eric would run, shouting with delight, "Mommy! Daddy! The terrorists are coming!"

Terrorists or tourists—without question, the Gingerbread House has given us the gift of a lifetime of memories.

MENU

SPECIAL OCCASION

COASTAL EMPIRE DINNER PARTY

Asparagus in Prosciutto

Hot Artichoke Dip

Baked Brie with Wild Mushrooms

Mandarin Orange and
Black Walnut Salad

Roasted Pork Tenderloin with
Dijon Cream Sauce or
Low Country
Pecan-Crusted Flounder

Baked Tomatoes Stuffed with Boursin

Almond Rice

Warm Sourdough Rolls

Apple and Green Tomato Preserve Pie

Whole Vanilla Bean Ice Cream

"Coastal Empire" is the phrase often used to
refer to Savannah. This menu is the essence of
elegant entertaining in Savannah—a combination
of delectable seafood and regional favorites
that will delight your palate!

CHICKEN MILANO

1 T. cooking oil
6 boneless, skinless chicken
   breast halves
Salt and pepper to taste
1 (12 oz.) jar spaghetti
   sauce mix

1 T. dried parsley flakes
6 slices Mozzarella or
   Monterey Jack cheese

Preheat oven to 350°. Heat oil in a large skillet; sprinkle chicken breasts with salt and pepper and lightly brown both sides of breasts. Place in a 9" x 13" baking dish and cover each breast with spaghetti sauce; sprinkle each with ½ teaspoon parsley flakes.

Bake for 30 minutes. Top each chicken breast with a slice of cheese; return to oven and bake 10 additional minutes. Remove from oven and serve immediately. *Yield: 6 servings.*

Dijon Chicken Breasts

2 tsp. Dijon mustard
3 T. grainy mustard
½ C. plain dry bread crumbs
½ tsp. salt
Black pepper to taste
6 boneless, skinless chicken
   breasts
2 T. olive oil

1 T. butter
2 C. thickly sliced mushrooms
3 green onions, thinly sliced
½ C. white wine
½ C. chicken broth
½ C. heavy cream
3-4 drops lemon juice

Mix mustards together in small bowl, reserving 1 tablespoon. Mix bread crumbs, salt and pepper in shallow bowl. Brush all but 1 tablespoon mustard over both sides of chicken breasts; coat with crumbs. Place in single layer on plate, cover with plastic wrap and refrigerate 30 minutes.

Preheat oven to 375°. Heat oil and butter in large skillet over medium-high heat. When foam subsides, add as much chicken as will fit in a single layer; sauté, turning once, until golden, about 4 minutes. Transfer to baking sheet. Repeat with remaining chicken, adding more oil if needed. Bake until chicken is cooked through, about 20-25 minutes.

Add mushrooms and all but 1 tablespoon green onions to skillet. Sauté until golden. Add wine and broth and simmer, scraping browned bits off bottom of pan, until reduced by half. Stir in cream and simmer until slightly thickened. Add reserved mustard. Increase heat to high and boil until thick. Add lemon juice and season to taste. Transfer chicken to serving platter. Pour sauce over chicken; sprinkle with remaining green onions. *Yield: 6 servings.*

CHICKEN CORDON BLEU

4 boneless, skinless chicken
  breasts
½ C. shredded Swiss cheese
¼ C. finely chopped ham
Salt to taste
2 tsp. Dijon mustard

1 egg
2 T. water
¼ C. flour
¼ tsp. salt
⅓ C. fine dry bread crumbs
Cooking oil

Place one chicken breast, boned side up, between two pieces of plastic wrap. Working from the center, pound lightly with meat mallet until about ⅛" thick. Repeat with remaining chicken breasts.

In a small bowl, combine cheese and ham. Sprinkle each breast with salt; spread with mustard. Divide cheese mixture into 4 parts, placing one fourth in the center of each breast. Fold in sides; roll up jelly roll fashion, pressing ends to seal. Secure with toothpicks.

In medium bowl, combine egg and water. Combine flour and ¼ teaspoon salt in shallow pan; coat chicken with flour mixture, then dip in egg mixture. Roll in bread crumbs; cover and refrigerate 1 hour.

Preheat oven to 375°. Heat ½ inch oil in large skillet; fry chicken rolls until golden brown. Remove toothpicks and place in baking dish. Bake 20-25 minutes. *Yield: 4 servings.*

Parsleyed Chicken en Croûte

2 T. margarine or butter
4 boneless, skinless chicken
  breast halves
Salt and pepper to taste
½ pkg. (17¼ oz. size) frozen
  puff pastry sheets

1 egg, beaten
1 T. water
1 (4 oz.) container herbed
  cream cheese spread
¼ C. chopped fresh parsley

In medium skillet over medium-high heat, melt margarine. Season chicken with salt and pepper, add to margarine and cook until browned. Remove chicken from skillet, cover and refrigerate 15 minutes or up to 24 hours.

Thaw pastry sheet at room temperature for 30 minutes; mix egg and water and set aside. Preheat oven to 400°.

Unfold pastry on a lightly floured surface. Roll into a 14" square and cut into four 7" squares. Spread about 2 tablespoons of the herbed cream cheese spread in the center of each square. Sprinkle with 1 tablespoon parsley and top with cooked chicken.

Brush edges of squares with egg mixture. Fold each corner to center on top of chicken and seal edges. Place seam side down on baking sheet. Brush with egg mixture.

Bake 25 minutes or until golden. *Yield: 4 servings.*

CHICKEN ROULADE IN PEPPER PESTO

4 boneless chicken breast halves	8 thin slices peppered salami
1/8 tsp. salt	4 tsp. grated Parmesan or Romano cheese
1 jar roasted red bell pepper, cut into 12 strips	1 T. olive oil
	Pepper Pesto (below)

Place chicken between 2 sheets of waxed paper and pound to about 1/4" thickness. Sprinkle lightly with salt, then top each breast with three strips red bell pepper and two overlapping slices salami. Sprinkle each with 1 teaspoon cheese and roll up the breasts.

Place chicken seam side down in a small baking dish, brush with olive oil. Bake at 350° for 25-30 minutes, basting occasionally, until chicken is fully cooked. Transfer chicken to a cutting board, cut crosswise into 1/2" slices and place on dinner plates. Spread Pepper Pesto around chicken. *Yield: 4 servings.*

PEPPER PESTO

2 large red bell peppers	1/4 tsp. salt
1/2 C. grated Parmesan cheese	1/4 tsp. white pepper
1/4 C. almonds	1/2 C. olive oil
2 small cloves garlic, halved	1/2-3/4 C. chicken broth

Place whole peppers on their sides on a large baking sheet. Bake at 500° for 20 minutes or until skin is blackened and charred. Transfer peppers immediately to a plastic bag and seal the top. Refrigerate 10 minutes or until peppers cool. Peel and seed peppers, discarding seeds and charred skin.

Position knife blade in food processor bowl; add peppers, cheese, almonds, garlic, salt and pepper. Process until smooth. With processor running, drizzle oil through food chute in a slow, steady stream until combined. Add chicken broth and pour into a saucepan; heat thoroughly. *Yield: 2 cups.*

CHEESE-STUFFED CHICKEN BREASTS

6 boneless, skinless chicken
   breasts
1 C. Ricotta cheese
½ C. shredded Cheddar cheese
½ C. grated Parmesan cheese
1 egg, beaten
¼ C. finely chopped pecans
1 T. parsley

¼ tsp. ground nutmeg
⅛ tsp. pepper
1 stick butter, melted
1½ C. fine bread crumbs
1 tsp. salt
¼ C. vegetable oil
2 T. butter

Placing each chicken breast between two pieces of waxed paper, use a meat mallet to flatten each breast to ¼" thickness. Combine Ricotta, Cheddar, Parmesan, egg, pecans, parsley, nutmeg and pepper; set aside. Place a heaping tablespoon of cheese mixture in the center of each breast; roll breast and secure with a toothpick.

Place melted butter in a pan or bowl. Mix together bread crumbs and salt, placing in a shallow bowl. Dip each chicken breast in butter, then roll in bread crumb mixture until lightly coated.

Heat vegetable oil and 2 tablespoons butter in a medium skillet. When butter has melted and foam subsides, place each breast in the oil; sauté until lightly browned on each side, about 3-4 minutes.

Remove toothpicks and place breasts, seam side down, in shallow baking dish; brush with melted butter. Bake, uncovered, at 350° for 40-45 minutes, basting occasionally. *Yield: 6 servings.*

PECAN-CRUSTED CHICKEN

½ C. flour
1 tsp. salt
6 chicken breast halves
1 egg, beaten

2 T. water
1 C. finely chopped pecans
¼ C. cooking oil
1 T. butter

Preheat oven to 350°. Mix flour and salt together; dredge each chicken breast half in flour mixture. Mix egg with water; dip each breast into egg mixture, then coat both sides with chopped pecans.

Heat oil and butter in a large skillet. Cook chicken 3-4 minutes, then turn to brown other side. Add more oil if necessary. Place breasts in a baking pan coated with vegetable spray. Bake, uncovered, for 25-30 minutes or until chicken is well cooked but tender. Remove from pan and serve immediately. *Yield: 6 servings.*

CHICKEN AND WILD RICE CASSEROLE

1 pkg. Uncle Ben's Long Grain
   and Wild Rice
½ C. chopped onion
½ C. chopped celery
2 T. butter
1 can condensed cream of
   mushroom soup

½ C. sour cream
⅓ C. white wine
½ tsp. curry powder
1 C. cubed cooked chicken

Prepare rice mix according to package directions. Meanwhile, cook onion and celery in butter until tender. Stir in soup, sour cream, wine and curry powder. Add chicken and cooked rice, stirring gently to mix.

Turn into casserole and bake, uncovered, at 350° for 35-40 minutes. *Yield: 6-8 servings.*

CHICKEN, BROCCOLI AND CREAM CHEESE CASSEROLE

6 boneless, skinless chicken
 breasts
2 (10 oz.) pkgs. frozen
 broccoli spears
2 (8 oz.) pkgs. cream cheese

2 C. milk
1 tsp. salt
¾-1 tsp. garlic salt
1½ C. grated Parmesan cheese

Preheat oven to 350°. Cook chicken breasts, slicing into thin strips. Cook broccoli spears and cut into small pieces and arrange in bottom of an 8½" x 11" casserole.

In a saucepan, soften cream cheese over low heat; add milk, salt, garlic salt and ¾ cup Parmesan, blending until smooth.

Pour 1 cup of sauce over broccoli. Top with chicken, then follow with the remaining sauce. Top with remaining ¾ cup Parmesan cheese. Bake for 25-30 minutes or until brown and bubbly; let stand 5-10 minutes, then serve. *Yield: 6-8 servings.*

BAKED CORNISH HENS

4 Cornish hens
Salt to taste
2 tsp. dried whole rosemary,
   crushed

Cornbread Dressing (p. 134)
4 skewers (5", wooden or
   metal)
1 stick butter, melted

Preheat oven to 350°. Remove giblets from hens; reserve for other uses. Rinse hens with cold water and pat dry. Salt each cavity, then sprinkle hens with rosemary.

Stuff hens with Cornbread Dressing. Seal the cavity by inserting a 5" skewer into one leg, through the skin covering the cavity, then out through the other leg.

Brush hens with melted butter. Bake for 1 hour, basting intermittently with butter or pan drippings, until meat thermometer registers 185°. *Yield: 4 servings.*

HONEY-GLAZED HAM

½ C. packed brown sugar
2 T. dry mustard
3 T. honey

2 tsp. pineapple juice
   (or orange juice)
1 (4-6 lb.) boneless ham

Stir brown sugar, dry mustard and honey together. Add enough pineapple juice to create a thick paste. Coat ham with mixture. Bake at 350° for 45 minutes, basting occasionally. *Yield: 8-10 servings.*

PORK LOIN ROAST WITH DIJON CREAM SAUCE

Salt and pepper to taste
1 (3 lb.) pork tenderloin
¼ C. butter
2 T. vegetable oil
3 green onions, chopped
⅓ C. dry white wine

⅓ C. Dijon mustard
½ C. heavy whipping cream
1 large firm ripe tomato,
    peeled, seeded and finely
    chopped, for garnish

Sprinkle salt and pepper on tenderloin, placing meat in a baking dish. Bake, uncovered, in a 350° oven until meat thermometer registers 175° (about 1½ hours). Melt butter and oil together in a large skillet. Add green onions and cook over low heat for 5 minutes. Increase heat, add wine and bring to a boil. Cook until mixture is reduced to a few syrupy spoonfuls. Whisk in the mustard and whipping cream and boil for 2 minutes. Taste and correct seasonings.

Remove tenderloin from oven and slice into 1" medallions. Arrange on dinner plates and pour sauce over each plate. Garnish with a small amount of chopped tomato. Serve immediately.
Yield: 6-8 servings.

Note: For a delicious alternative, substitute an 8-ounce jar of mango chutney for the Dijon cream sauce. To serve, spoon approximately 3 tablespoons of room-temperature chutney over each serving of medallions. Garnish with fresh rosemary or parsley.

Another spicy alternative accompaniment for pork tenderloin is barbecue chili butter (see recipe, p. 59). To serve, top each medallion with a dollop of chili butter.

Low Country Bacon and Egg Casserole

½ C. butter
½ C. flour
4 C. half and half (or, for thinner sauce, 2 C. half and half plus 2 C. milk)
½ C. chopped parsley
2 lbs. grated Cheddar cheese
1 clove garlic, minced
2 dozen hard-boiled eggs, sliced and divided into 3 parts
1½ lbs. bacon, fried crisp, drained, crumbled and divided into 3 parts
Buttered bread crumbs (optional)

Melt butter in saucepan; add flour and mix until smooth. Add half and half or milk, parsley, cheese and garlic. Cook, stirring constantly, until mixture thickens.

Remove from heat. Layer sauce, eggs and bacon in two greased 11" x 13" pans, beginning and ending with sauce. Sprinkle top with buttered bread crumbs, if desired.

Bake in 350° oven 30 minutes or until brown and bubbly.
Yield: 20 servings.

VEAL MARSALA

4 veal cutlets
1 T. cooking oil
1 T. butter
1 clove garlic, minced
1 T. tomato paste

½ C. dry red Marsala
½ C. red wine
½ lb. small fresh mushroom
   caps
1 tsp. chopped parsley

Pound veal cutlets into ¼" thickness, if necessary. Heat oil and butter in heavy skillet. Brown cutlets on both sides; remove from pan.

Add garlic to pan and sauté briefly. Mix tomato paste with wines; add to pan, along with mushrooms. Stir to blend with pan juices. Simmer 3-5 minutes.

Return cutlets to pan and heat through. Sprinkle with parsley and serve immediately. *Yield: 4 servings.*

FILET MIGNON WITH DIJON COGNAC SAUCE

Fresh ground pepper
4 (1¼" thick) beef filet mignon
   steaks
2 T. butter
2 T. vegetable oil
Salt

2 green onions, minced
2 T. Cognac
⅔ C. whipping cream
1 tsp. Dijon mustard
Fresh parsley or rosemary
   sprigs for garnish

Sprinkle pepper generously over both sides of steaks and press in.

Melt 1 tablespoon butter with 2 tablespoons oil in heavy medium skillet over high heat. Salt steaks on one side and add to skillet, salted side down. Cook until brown, about 2 minutes. Salt tops, turn and cook until second sides are brown.

Reduce heat to medium and cook to desired degree of doneness, turning occasionally, about 6 minutes for rare. Transfer steaks to heated plates and set aside.

Discard drippings from skillet. Add remaining 1 tablespoon butter to same skillet and melt over medium heat. Add green onions and cook, stirring, 1 minute.

Remove from heat and add Cognac. Return to heat and whisk in whipping cream and Dijon mustard; cook over medium heat until sauce has thickened.

Ladle sauce over steaks and garnish with fresh parsley or rosemary sprigs. Serve immediately. *Yield: 4 servings.*

BEEF STROGANOFF

1½ lbs. sirloin steak, about
   ¾" thick
1 medium onion, chopped
2 cloves garlic, minced
1 (4 oz.) can sliced
   mushrooms, drained

1½ tsp. salt
¼ tsp. pepper
1 C. beef bouillon
3 T. tomato paste
¾ C. sour cream mixed with
   2 T. flour

Cut sirloin steak in ¾" cubes; brown in large skillet. Add onion, garlic and mushrooms. Sauté until onion is golden brown and mushrooms are tender.

Add remaining ingredients except sour cream and flour. Lower heat and simmer for 1 hour. Stir in sour cream and flour mixture and cook for an additional 15 minutes, stirring frequently.

Serve over rice or egg noodles. *Yield: 4-5 servings.*

BEEF TENDERLOIN TIPS WITH MUSHROOMS AND ONIONS

1 stick butter, room temperature	1 large onion, sliced
1 clove garlic, minced	½ lb. mushrooms, sliced
1 T. white wine	1 lb. beef tenderloin tips
1 tsp. chopped fresh parsley	Salt, pepper and garlic powder to taste
⅛ tsp. pepper	Dash sherry

Make garlic butter by combining first five ingredients in a bowl; thoroughly blend on low speed with electric mixer. Melt 2 tablespoons garlic butter in large skillet over medium-high heat; add onion, sauté until tender. Add mushrooms and cook lightly. Transfer to plate and keep warm; drain and wipe pan.

Season meat with salt, pepper and garlic powder. Melt 1 tablespoon garlic butter in the same skillet over medium-high heat. Add meat and sauté to desired doneness. Return onion and mushrooms to pan; stir to blend. Add sherry, top with additional garlic butter and serve immediately. *Yield: 4-6 servings.*

STEAK AU POIVRE

1 T. coarsely ground pepper
20 oz. boneless beef sirloin
   steak
4 tsp. butter

1 tsp. salt
2 C. mushrooms, sliced
2 T. minced shallots
¼ C. red wine

Press pepper into each side of meat; let stand 15 minutes. Place meat on rack of broiling pan and broil in preheated oven 3 inches from heat until rare, about 2 minutes on each side.

In a medium skillet, heat butter over high heat until bubbly. Transfer meat to skillet and quickly sear on both sides. Sprinkle each side with ½ teaspoon salt. Remove meat to warmed serving platter; set aside and keep warm. In the same skillet, combine mushrooms and shallots; sauté until mushrooms are golden, about 1 minute. Add wine and cook, stirring constantly, until liquid is slightly reduced, about 3 minutes. Pour sauce over meat and serve immediately. *Yield: 4 servings.*

ROAST BEEF IN SOUR CREAM SAUCE

1 (3½-4 lb.) boneless rump
  roast
2 T. vegetable oil
½ C. water
2 cubes beef bouillon
1 bay leaf
½ tsp. salt
½ tsp. black pepper

2 onions, quartered
2 carrots, scraped and
  cut into pieces
2 T. all-purpose flour
3 T. water
8 oz. sour cream
Hot cooked noodles

Brown roast on all sides in hot oil in a large Dutch oven. Combine ½ cup water and bouillon cubes; add to Dutch oven. Add bay leaf, salt and pepper. Cover, reduce heat and simmer 2½ hours. Add onions and carrots; cover and cook 30 minutes or until vegetables and meat are tender.

Remove roast and vegetables from Dutch oven; keep warm. Remove bay leaf and discard.

Combine flour and 3 tablespoons water; stir into pan drippings. Cook, stirring constantly, until gravy is smooth and thickened. Add sour cream and vegetables to gravy. Cook, stirring constantly, until thoroughly heated.

Place cooked noodles on a serving platter. Slice roast and arrange over noodles. Serve with gravy. *Yield: 6-8 servings.*

CHEDDAR MEATBALLS

1 lb. ground beef
¼ C. fine dry bread crumbs
¼ C. finely chopped onion
1 egg, slightly beaten

¼ tsp. salt
1 can Cheddar cheese soup
½ C. water
2 T. chopped parsley

Mix ground beef, bread crumbs, onion, egg and salt. Shape into 20 meatballs. In skillet, brown meatballs; pour off fat. Stir in soup, water and parsley.

Cover; cook over low heat 20 minutes or until done, stirring occasionally. Serve over rice or egg noodles. *Yield: 4 servings.*

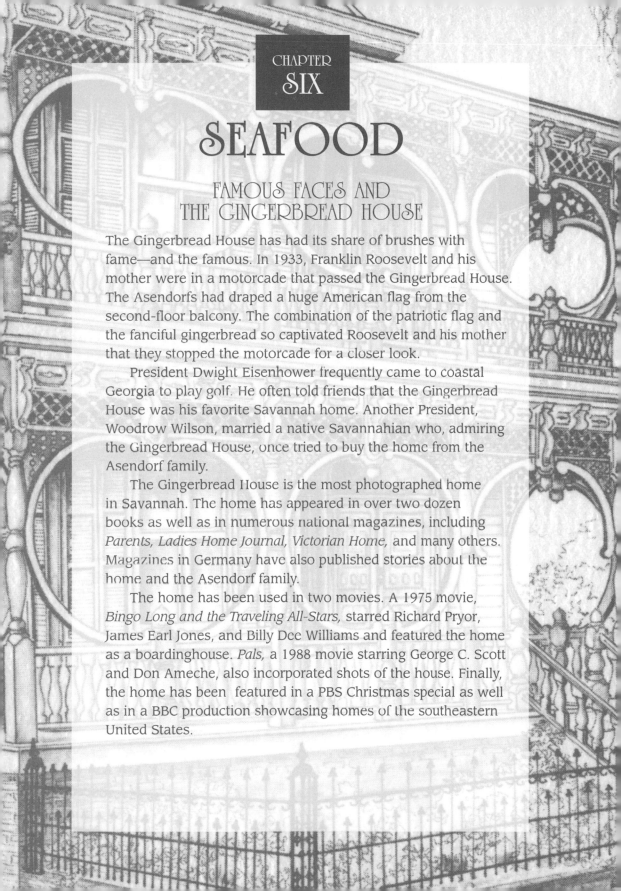

SEAFOOD

FAMOUS FACES AND THE GINGERBREAD HOUSE

The Gingerbread House has had its share of brushes with fame—and the famous. In 1933, Franklin Roosevelt and his mother were in a motorcade that passed the Gingerbread House. The Asendorfs had draped a huge American flag from the second-floor balcony. The combination of the patriotic flag and the fanciful gingerbread so captivated Roosevelt and his mother that they stopped the motorcade for a closer look.

President Dwight Eisenhower frequently came to coastal Georgia to play golf. He often told friends that the Gingerbread House was his favorite Savannah home. Another President, Woodrow Wilson, married a native Savannahian who, admiring the Gingerbread House, once tried to buy the home from the Asendorf family.

The Gingerbread House is the most photographed home in Savannah. The home has appeared in over two dozen books as well as in numerous national magazines, including *Parents, Ladies Home Journal, Victorian Home,* and many others. Magazines in Germany have also published stories about the home and the Asendorf family.

The home has been used in two movies. A 1975 movie, *Bingo Long and the Traveling All-Stars,* starred Richard Pryor, James Earl Jones, and Billy Dee Williams and featured the home as a boardinghouse. *Pals,* a 1988 movie starring George C. Scott and Don Ameche, also incorporated shots of the house. Finally, the home has been featured in a PBS Christmas special as well as in a BBC production showcasing homes of the southeastern United States.

MENU

SPECIAL OCCASION

LOW COUNTRY BOIL

Low Country Shrimp Boil

Dixie Cole Slaw

Smoky Baked Beans

Creamy Potato Salad

Country Biscuits

Hushpuppies

Cream Cheese Brownies

Sweet Clove Tea and
Assorted Beverages

A Low Country boil provides the perfect excuse
for getting together, and as such is a long-standing
Savannah tradition. This is usually an outdoor event,
often with picnic tables, red checkered tablecloths,
casual dress, and generous portions of food.

SHRIMP IN LEMON BUTTER

1 C. butter
¼ C. lemon juice
1 clove garlic, minced
1 tsp. parsley flakes
1 tsp. Worcestershire sauce
1 tsp. soy sauce
½ tsp. coarsely ground
   black pepper

¼ tsp. salt
¼ tsp. garlic salt
2 lbs. large shrimp, peeled and
   deveined
Lemon wedges (optional)

Melt butter in a large skillet. Add next eight ingredients; bring
to a boil. Add shrimp; cook over medium heat 5 minutes, stirring
occasionally. Garnish shrimp with lemon wedges, if desired.
Yield: 4-6 servings.

JAMBALAYA

2 onions, chopped
2 stalks celery, chopped
¼ green bell pepper, chopped
4 cloves garlic, chopped
¼ C. butter
1 (28 oz.) can tomatoes
1 (6 oz.) can tomato paste
1 tsp. chopped parsley

½ tsp. thyme
1 lb. deli ham, diced
2 lbs. shrimp, cooked, peeled
   and deveined
3 C. cooked yellow rice
Salt, black pepper and
   cayenne pepper to taste

Sauté onions, celery, bell pepper and garlic in butter for 5 minutes. Add tomatoes and tomato paste. Cook 5 minutes, stirring constantly. Add parsley and thyme.

Cook 30 minutes, stirring frequently. Stir in ham and shrimp; cook 5 minutes. Stir in rice, season to taste and simmer 30 minutes, stirring often. *Yield: 8 servings.*

SHRIMP CREOLE

2 T. butter
½ C. chopped onion
1 bay leaf, crushed
¼ C. diced celery
1 tsp. minced parsley
½ C. chopped bell pepper

⅛ tsp. cayenne pepper
1 tsp. salt
1 (6 oz.) can tomato paste
2½ C. water
2 C. seasoned cooked shrimp

Melt butter over low heat. Add onion, bay leaf and celery and cook until tender. Blend in remaining ingredients except shrimp. Cook slowly, stirring occasionally, about 30 minutes. Stir in shrimp. Serve over hot cooked rice. *Yield: 6 servings.*

SHRIMP STEAMED IN BEER

5 lbs. shrimp in shell
12 leaves Boston lettuce
2 (12 oz.) cans beer

¾ C. (1½ sticks) butter, melted
4 cloves garlic, minced

Wash shrimp. In a large steamer, layer shrimp and lettuce; pour beer over top. Cover and heat to boiling. Steam shrimp 20-25 minutes or until pink.

Drain shrimp, reserving ½ cup liquid. In a small bowl, combine reserved liquid, melted butter and garlic.

Arrange shrimp and lettuce leaves on serving platter. Serve with melted butter sauce. *Yield: 6-8 servings.*

LOW COUNTRY SHRIMP BOIL

6 lbs. raw shrimp (medium to large), in shells
5 lbs. Italian sausage (½ sweet, ½ hot)
1 stick butter
¼ C. salt

½ C. seafood seasoning (Zatarain's, Old Bay or other brand)
2 lbs. small red new potatoes
12 ears sweet corn, broken in half

Wash and rinse shrimp. Cut Italian sausage into 2-3" lengths.

Fill a 3-gallon pot half full of water. Add 1 stick butter, salt and seafood seasoning; bring to a boil. Add sausage and boil approximately 10 minutes. Add potatoes and cook another 5 minutes, then put corn in water and boil an additional 5 minutes. Add shrimp, boiling 5-7 minutes or until shrimp is pink and shells begin to separate.

Drain and serve from one large bowl. Place side bowls on the serving table containing Seafood Cocktail Sauce for the shrimp (see recipe, page 58) and melted butter for the corn and potatoes. *Yield: 12-15 servings.*

SHRIMP AND CRAB CASSEROLE

¼ C. butter
¼ C. flour
½ pt. whipping cream
Pinch salt and pepper
¼ C. sherry

½ lb. white crab meat
½ lb. medium shrimp, peeled
 and deveined
1 C. grated sharp Cheddar
 cheese

Make a cream sauce with butter, flour and whipping cream. Add salt, pepper and sherry to cream sauce. Remove from heat. Add crab meat and shrimp.

Pour mixture into buttered casserole or individual baking dishes. Sprinkle with grated cheese and bake in hot oven until cheese melts. *Yield: 4 servings.*

DEVILED CRAB

1 lb. crab meat	½ C. bacon drippings
1½ C. soft bread crumbs	1½ tsp. Dijon mustard
½ tsp. ground thyme	¼ C. Worcestershire sauce
¾ C. minced bell pepper	1 egg, beaten
¾ C. minced celery	1 C. ground salted crackers

Make sure crab meat is free of shell particles, then mix with bread crumbs and thyme. Sauté bell pepper and celery in bacon drippings until tender, about 3 minutes, then add to crab mixture. Add mustard, Worcestershire and egg, mixing thoroughly.

Place in individual casseroles or 1½-quart buttered casserole. Sprinkle with cracker meal.

Bake in preheated 350° oven for 45-60 minutes, until crab is browned on top. Serve hot or at room temperature.
Yield: 4 servings.

CRAB NEWBURG

2 T. margarine or butter
1/3 C. diced green pepper
1/3 C. sliced mushrooms
2 T. chopped parsley
2 T. flour
Salt to taste
1/4 tsp. dry mustard

Pinch cayenne pepper
1 C. milk
2 T. white wine
2 (1 lb. each) cans crab meat,
   drained
2 T. grated Parmesan cheese

Preheat oven to 350°. Melt margarine and butter in a saucepan. Add green pepper, mushrooms and parsley; sauté until pepper and mushrooms are tender.

In a bowl, combine flour, salt, dry mustard and cayenne pepper. Blend into sautéed mixture. Add milk and wine; stir until thickened.

Place crab meat in seashells, pastry shells, or a casserole and cover with sauce. Sprinkle with Parmesan cheese and bake 8-12 minutes. *Yield: 6-8 servings.*

CRAB IMPERIAL

½ C. butter
2 T. chopped green onions
1 T. finely chopped green
  pepper
1 T. finely chopped red pepper
2 T. flour
¼ tsp. salt
½ tsp. celery salt
½ tsp. white pepper

1 C. half and half
2 T. dry sherry
Dash Tabasco
1 egg
1 lb. crab meat
1 T. parsley flakes
1 (3 oz.) jar chopped pimiento
1 C. soft bread crumbs
2 T. butter, melted

Melt ½ cup butter in a large saucepan; add green onions, green and red peppers and sauté until vegetables are tender. Mix together flour, salt, celery salt and white pepper, then stir into butter. Add half and half and cook, stirring, over medium heat until mixture thickens. Remove from heat and add sherry and Tabasco.

In a medium bowl, beat egg slightly. Add a small amount of the hot, creamed mixture and beat into egg; this will prevent the egg from cooking. Return entire mixture to the saucepan and stir in crab meat, parsley and pimiento.

Pour mixture into a 9" x 13" baking pan. Top with bread crumbs and melted butter. Bake in preheated 350° oven for 30 minutes or until top is brown and bubbly and casserole is firm. Serve warm.
Yield: 4-6 servings.

Note: May also be used as an appetizer, served with water crackers, toast points or phyllo cups.

SCALLOPS WITH GINGER IN PUFF PASTRY

1 pkg. frozen puff pastry
  shells, thawed
1 C. white wine
2 shallots, minced
2 tsp. ginger
1½ lbs. bay scallops
6 T. heavy cream

1 C. (2 sticks) unsalted butter,
  cut into pieces
Salt and pepper to taste
2 tsp. fresh lemon juice
3 green onions, cut into
  thin slices

Cook puff pastry according to package directions. Combine wine, shallots and ginger in medium saucepan; bring to a boil, stirring occasionally. Add scallops and cream; cook 2 minutes.

Remove scallops using slotted spoon. Increase heat and cook liquid until reduced to 4 tablespoons, adding any juices drained from scallops. Whisk in all but 2 teaspoons butter, one piece at a time. Season with salt and pepper. Add lemon juice; set sauce aside.

Melt remaining butter in a small skillet over high heat; add green onions and cook 30 seconds; set aside. Stir scallops into sauce and heat through.

Reheat pastry shells in oven for 2 minutes. Place pastry shells on heated plates and fill with scallop mixture. Sprinkle with green onions and serve immediately. *Yield: 4 servings.*

SALMON FILLETS IN CRUSTY POTATOES

4 salmon fillets
2 tsp. thyme
Salt and pepper to taste
2 large potatoes, sliced
  wafer thin

¼ C. butter
Tomato Dill Sauce (p. 115)
Fresh dill for garnish

Sprinkle each salmon fillet with thyme, salt and pepper. Place a thin layer of potato slices on top of each fillet, overlapping slices slightly to cover the entire surface of the salmon. (Potatoes should have a "feathered" look created by the overlap.)

Place a 6" x 12" piece of plastic wrap on top of each fillet, thus covering potato slices and salmon. Placing one hand on the plastic wrap for support, flip the fillet over to the underneath side. The plastic wrap should now be between the salmon and the work surface.

Repeat the process of sprinkling thyme, salt and pepper on the remaining side of each fillet, then cover with a thin layer of potatoes, overlapped as before.

In saucepan, melt butter. Use plastic wrap to flip each fillet onto a spatula, then use spatula to slide fillet into the saucepan. Sauté each fillet until potatoes are brown and crusty (3-4 minutes); turn and sauté other side an additional 3-4 minutes until salmon is flaky. Add more butter if necessary.

When finished, set aside or place in slightly warm oven; do not cover or potatoes will become soggy. Prepare Tomato Dill Sauce. Place a large spoonful of sauce on a dinner plate, spreading to create a thin coating. Place salmon on top of sauce. Garnish with fresh dill and serve immediately. *Yield: 4 servings.*

TOMATO DILL SAUCE

2 T. chopped onions
2 T. butter
2 medium fresh tomatoes,
   coarsely chopped

½ tsp. minced garlic
¼ tsp. dill
¼ tsp. salt

Sauté onions in butter until onions are translucent; add tomatoes, garlic, dill and salt. Cook on stove top just until tomatoes begin to become tender; do not overcook. *Yield: ¾ cup.*

SALMON WITH LEMON BUTTER

6 salmon fillets
1 T. butter
½ C. white wine
¼ C. lemon juice

¼ tsp. salt
1 stick butter
⅛ tsp. white pepper
1 T. chopped fresh chives

Preheat oven to 350°. Butter 9" x 13" baking dish; place fillets in a single layer in the dish. Pour wine over fillets. Bake, uncovered, for 15-18 minutes, basting frequently with wine, until salmon flakes easily with a fork. While salmon is baking, heat lemon juice and salt in a small saucepan until just boiling. Add 1 stick butter, whisking until mixture is creamy. Stir in white pepper.

Spoon lemon butter over fillets and top with fresh chives. Serve any remaining sauce on the side. *Yield: 6 servings.*

COLD POACHED SALMON WITH CUCUMBER CREAM

1 ¼ C. clam juice
1 ½ C. white wine
2 C. water
4 salmon fillets, skinned
1 T. vegetable oil

1 tsp. lemon juice
1 small cucumber, peeled,
    halved, seeded and
    thinly sliced

In a medium skillet, bring clam juice, wine and 2 cups water to a boil. Reduce heat to a simmer and add salmon fillets. Add extra boiling water to cover salmon, if necessary. Poach until just opaque throughout, about 6 minutes.

Using a slotted spatula, transfer fillets to a serving platter and let cool.

In a small bowl, stir together oil and lemon juice. Brush this mixture over fillets. When cool, garnish with cucumber slices in overlapping fish scale pattern. Serve with Cucumber Cream (recipe follows). *Yield: 4 servings.*

CUCUMBER CREAM

¾ C. sour cream
¼ C. minced scallions
⅔ C. peeled, seeded and sliced
    cucumber

1 ½ T. lemon juice
Dash hot sauce, or to taste
¼ tsp. salt

In a medium bowl, stir together the sour cream, scallions, cucumber, lemon juice, hot sauce and salt. Cover with plastic wrap and refrigerate for up to 4 hours before serving. *Yield: 1 ½ cups.*

SNAPPER WITH GARLIC SAUCE

2 egg yolks	1 C. plus 1½ T. olive oil
2 T. white wine vinegar	½ C. ground walnuts
1 T. lemon juice	⅓ C. minced fresh parsley
2 cloves garlic, crushed	4 red snapper fillets, skinned
¾ tsp. salt	Lemon wedges for garnish

Process egg yolks, vinegar, lemon juice, garlic and salt in a blender until smooth. With the machine on, gradually pour in 1 cup olive oil in a thin, steady stream until oil is thoroughly incorporated and sauce thickens. Scrape into a small mixing bowl; stir in nuts and parsley. Set aside.

Preheat broiler. Brush fillets lightly on both sides with remaining 1½ tablespoons oil and broil 4 inches from heat, without turning, for about 4½ minutes or until fish separates easily when tested with a spoon.

Transfer fillets to 4 plates and salt lightly. Spoon several tablespoons of sauce over each fillet, garnish with lemon wedges and serve immediately. Pass remaining sauce separately. *Yield: 4 servings.*

GRILLED SNAPPER

1 tsp. oregano
1 tsp. basil
1 tsp. Creole seasoning
½ tsp. garlic powder
½ tsp. pepper
½ tsp. Italian seasoning

6 snapper fillets
½ C. white wine
¼ C. olive oil
12 slices bacon, partially
  cooked
Vegetable cooking spray

Combine oregano, basil, Creole seasoning, garlic powder, pepper and Italian seasoning in a small bowl; mix well. Divide mixture in half, setting half aside. Sprinkle remaining half on fish fillets. Place fillets in a shallow baking dish; pour wine over fillets. Cover and marinate in refrigerator 12 hours, turning fillets occasionally.

Drain fillets; rub both sides with olive oil and sprinkle evenly with reserved seasoning mixture. Wrap 2 slices bacon around each fillet; secure with wooden picks.

Spray a fish basket with cooking spray; place fish in basket. Grill fish over medium-hot coals 7-10 minutes on each side, or until fish flakes easily when tested with a fork. Remove fish from grill; remove picks. Serve immediately. *Yield: 6 servings.*

LOW COUNTRY
PECAN-CRUSTED FLOUNDER

1½ C. pecans, finely chopped	2 eggs, lightly beaten
1½ C. fresh bread crumbs	2 T. milk
½ tsp. salt	6 flounder fillets
¼ tsp. fresh ground pepper	3 T. butter
1 C. all-purpose flour	3 T. safflower oil

In a small bowl, combine pecans, bread crumbs, salt and pepper. Pour onto a large plate. Pour flour onto another large plate. In a large bowl, whisk together eggs and milk until blended.

Pat flounder dry and dredge, one piece at a time, in the flour, making sure to coat evenly. Shake off excess. Dip each fillet in the egg mixture and let any excess drain off. Coat the fillets in the pecan/bread crumb mixture, patting gently to help coating adhere. Shake off excess.

In a large skillet, melt 1½ tablespoons of the butter and 1½ tablespoons of the oil over moderate heat. Sauté 3 fillets until golden brown, about 3 minutes. Turn and sauté until golden brown on the other side.

Finish remaining fillets with remaining butter and oil. Serve hot.
Yield: 6 servings.

FLOUNDER CAESAR

1 lb. flounder fillets	½ C. (2 oz.) shredded Cheddar
½ C. golden Caesar salad	cheese
dressing	
1 C. butter cracker crumbs	

Preheat oven to 400°. Arrange fillets in a single layer in a lightly greased 9" x 13" baking dish. Drizzle dressing over fillets; sprinkle cracker crumbs over top.

Bake for 10 minutes; top with cheese and bake an additional 5 minutes or until fish flakes easily when tested with a fork. *Yield: 4 servings.*

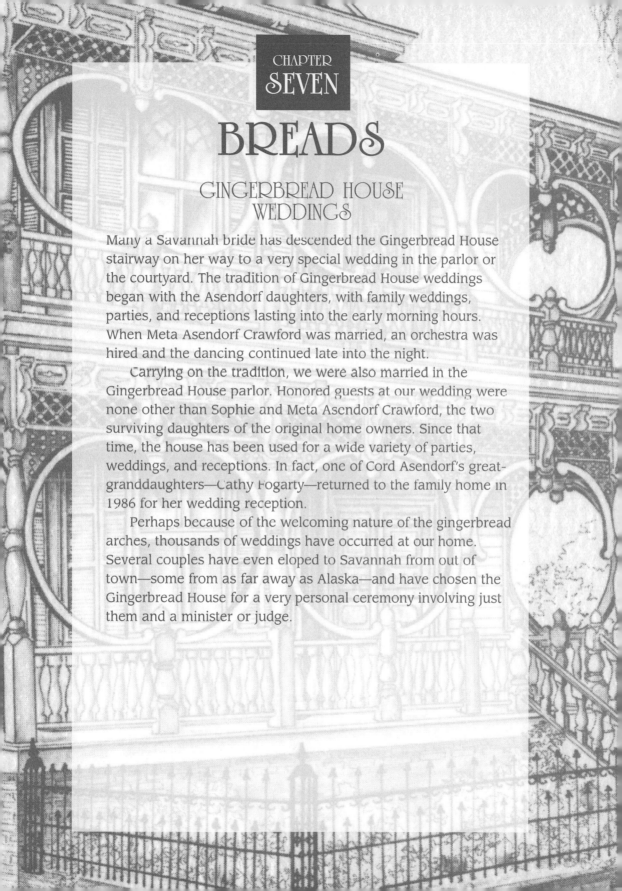

BREADS

GINGERBREAD HOUSE WEDDINGS

Many a Savannah bride has descended the Gingerbread House stairway on her way to a very special wedding in the parlor or the courtyard. The tradition of Gingerbread House weddings began with the Asendorf daughters, with family weddings, parties, and receptions lasting into the early morning hours. When Meta Asendorf Crawford was married, an orchestra was hired and the dancing continued late into the night.

Carrying on the tradition, we were also married in the Gingerbread House parlor. Honored guests at our wedding were none other than Sophie and Meta Asendorf Crawford, the two surviving daughters of the original home owners. Since that time, the house has been used for a wide variety of parties, weddings, and receptions. In fact, one of Cord Asendorf's great-granddaughters—Cathy Fogarty—returned to the family home in 1986 for her wedding reception.

Perhaps because of the welcoming nature of the gingerbread arches, thousands of weddings have occurred at our home. Several couples have even eloped to Savannah from out of town—some from as far away as Alaska—and have chosen the Gingerbread House for a very personal ceremony involving just them and a minister or judge.

MENU

SPECIAL OCCASION

WEDDING RECEPTION

Chicken Nuggets Italiano

Sirloin Teriyaki

Marinated Shrimp and Snow Peas

Sausage-Stuffed Mushrooms

Crab Imperial with Toast Points

Spinach-Stuffed Phyllo Bites

Stuffed Salami Cones

Fresh Vegetables with
Herbed Carrot Vegetable Dip

Miniature Carrot Cakes

Sunny Southern Fruit Punch

After years of working with brides, we have learned
that wedding receptions vary greatly from one region of
the country to another. This menu represents a typical
Savannah reception—a heavy hors d'oeuvres buffet
that provides good food and an opportunity for guests
to munch, mix, and mingle. Although this menu is
often used for Gingerbread House wedding receptions,
it is appropriate for any festive occasion.

DILLED ONION BREAD

1 medium onion, chopped
1 T. butter
1 pkg. dry yeast
¼ C. warm water
⅔ C. milk
¼ C. shortening

2 T. sugar
1½ tsp. salt
3-3¼ C. flour
1 tsp. dill seed
1 egg
Melted butter

Cook onion in 1 tablespoon butter until tender but not brown. Soften yeast in warm water.

Combine milk, shortening, sugar and salt. Stir in 1 cup flour; beat well. Add yeast, onion, dill seed and egg; mix well. Add enough flour to make a moderate stiff dough. Turn out on lightly floured board; knead dough until smooth and satiny.

Shape into a ball. Place in greased bowl, cover and let rise until double. Punch down, cover and let rise 10 minutes.

Shape into a loaf and place in greased pan. Brush top with melted butter. Let rise to double. Bake in preheated 375° oven 40 minutes or until done. *Yield: 1 loaf.*

COUNTRY BISCUITS

2 C. self-rising flour
⅓ C. shortening
¾ C. milk

3 T. butter or margarine,
  melted

Place flour in a bowl; cut in shortening with a pastry blender until mixture resembles coarse meal. Add milk and stir until dry ingredients are moistened. Turn dough out onto a lightly floured surface; knead 5 times.

Roll dough to ½" thickness; cut with a 1½" biscuit cutter. Place on a lightly greased baking sheet and bake at 450° for 12-14 minutes or until lightly browned.

Remove from oven; brush tops with melted butter. Serve warm. *Yield: 12 biscuits.*

LOW COUNTRY CORNBREAD

¾ C. self-rising yellow
  cornmeal
¾ C. self-rising flour
1½ tsp. baking powder

¼ C. sugar
1 C. milk
1 egg
¼ C. butter, melted

Preheat oven to 425°. Grease and flour an 8" square pan.

Combine dry ingredients in a medium mixing bowl. Whisk in milk, egg and melted butter.

Pour batter into prepared pan, then place in oven. Bake 25-30 minutes or until golden brown. *Yield: 16 large pieces.*

Italian Bread Sticks

4 C. bread flour
¼ C. sugar
1½ tsp. salt
1 pkg. dry yeast
1¼ C. milk

5 T. butter
2 tsp. dried basil leaves
½ tsp. celery seeds
¼ tsp. poultry seasoning

Combine 1 cup flour, sugar, salt and yeast in a large mixing bowl; set aside. Combine milk and 3 tablespoons butter in a small saucepan; heat until warm. Gradually add milk to dry ingredients, beating at low speed with an electric mixer. Beat 2 minutes at medium speed, scraping sides of bowl occasionally. Add ¾ cup flour, basil, celery seeds and poultry seasoning; beat at high speed 2 minutes. Stir in remaining flour as needed to make a soft dough.

Turn dough onto a lightly floured surface and knead 8 minutes or until smooth and elastic. Place dough in well-greased bowl, turning to grease top. Cover and let rise in a warm place, free from drafts, 1½ hours.

Punch dough down and turn out onto a lightly floured surface. Divide dough into 24 equal portions. Roll each portion into a 9" rope and place on greased baking sheet. Cover and repeat rising procedure until doubled in bulk.

Melt remaining 2 tablespoons butter; brush tops of bread sticks. Bake at 400° for 8-10 minutes or until golden brown. *Yield: 24 sticks.*

BRITTLE BREAD

½ C. butter or margarine
2¾ C. plain flour, sifted
¼ C. sugar

½ tsp. salt
½ tsp. baking soda
8 oz. plain yogurt

Cut butter into dry ingredients. Add yogurt until it makes a soft dough. Refrigerate.

Break off marble-size pieces and roll out on floured board or roll thin and cut into strips with a knife. Sprinkle with salt or sugar or leave plain.

Cook for 6-8 minutes in a 400° oven on an ungreased pan. After cooking, put bread back in a pan, turn oven off and place bread back in the oven; leave overnight.

This bread is excellent with dips, especially spinach dip. It will keep for a long time in an airtight tin. *Yield: 4 dinner servings; 20 appetizer servings.*

Note: Can use self-rising flour, but eliminate the baking soda and salt.

This is an old Savannah recipe passed down through several generations. The recipe was given to us by Mrs. Mimi Roberts.

BANANA NUT BREAD

2 medium, ripe bananas
1 tsp. lemon juice
½ C. butter
⅔ C. sugar
2 eggs

1¾ C. flour
2¼ tsp. baking powder
½ tsp. salt
⅔ C. pecans or walnuts,
    coarsely chopped

Preheat oven to 350°. Mash bananas until smooth, then add lemon juice; set aside.

Cream butter and sugar together. Add eggs, one at a time, followed by bananas. Sift dry ingredients together; add to creamed mixture, being careful not to overbeat. Stir in nuts.

Pour into greased loaf pan. Bake for 1 hour or until a knife inserted in the center comes out clean. Cool for 10 minutes, then remove from pan. *Yield: 1 loaf.*

CRANBERRY TEA BREAD

2 C. all-purpose flour
2 tsp. baking powder
¼ tsp. salt
¼ C. cold, unsalted butter,
  cut into small pieces
¾ C. plus 1 T. sugar

4 oz. chopped pecans
1 T. grated orange zest
1 egg
⅔ C. orange juice
2 C. fresh cranberries
1 T. milk

Preheat oven to 350°. Butter a 9" x 5" loaf pan; line bottom with waxed paper, then butter the paper. In a large bowl, mix together flour, baking powder and salt. Cut in butter until mixture resembles fine bread crumbs. Add ¾ cup sugar, pecans and orange zest; toss to blend.

In a small bowl, beat egg with a fork until frothy. Beat in orange juice. Pour this liquid over dry ingredients and stir just until dough begins to mass together. Before all the flour is thoroughly incorporated, add cranberries and stir them into the dough until evenly distributed.

Scrape batter into prepared pan and spread evenly with a spatula. Brush milk evenly over surface of batter and sprinkle remaining 1 tablespoon sugar on top.

Bake in middle of oven for 1 hour and 15 minutes, or until loaf is well risen, golden brown and crusty and a tester inserted in the center comes out clean. Transfer loaf to a rack to cool for 20 minutes.

Run a thick knife around inside of pan and invert loaf onto rack. Peel off waxed paper and turn loaf right side up; let cool completely. Put loaf in a tin with a tight-fitting lid and set aside overnight.
Yield: 1 loaf.

ZUCCHINI BREAD

2 C. white sugar
1 C. packed brown sugar
¾ C. margarine
¾ C. cooking oil
3 eggs
4½ C. all-purpose flour
½ tsp. baking powder

1 tsp. baking soda
1½ tsp. cinnamon
4½ tsp. vanilla
3 C. grated zucchini
1½ T. grated orange peel
¾ C. raisins
¾ C. nuts

The last 3 ingredients are optional. Mix all ingredients together in the order given. The zucchini should be cored but can either be peeled or grated as is; a food processor with grating attachment works well for this.

Preheat oven to 325°. Pour mixture into 2 greased loaf pans. Bake for 1 hour, or until knife inserted in center comes out clean. Cool before cutting. *Yield: 2 loaves.*

PUMPKIN BREAD

3 C. sugar
4 eggs
⅔ C. water
1 tsp. cinnamon
3⅓ C. flour

1 C. cooking oil
2 C. cooked pumpkin
1½ tsp. salt
1 tsp. nutmeg
2 tsp. baking soda

Combine all ingredients, in order given, and mix with electric mixer. Divide dough into quantities for 3 small or 2 large bread pans. Grease pans, add dough and bake 1 hour at 350° or until knife inserted in center comes out clean. Bread freezes well. *Yield: 3 small or 2 large loaves.*

PEACH MUFFINS

2 C. unsifted all-purpose flour	¼ tsp. ground nutmeg
⅔ C. sugar	¾ C. milk
1 T. baking powder	¼ C. butter, melted
½ tsp. salt	1 large egg, slightly beaten
½ tsp. ground cinnamon	½ C. chopped fresh peaches

Preheat oven to 425°. Grease twelve 2½" muffin pan cups. In a large bowl, combine flour, sugar, baking powder, salt, cinnamon and nutmeg.

In a 2-cup glass measuring cup, stir together milk, butter and egg. Add milk mixture to flour mixture. Stir just until dry ingredients are completely moistened. Batter should be lumpy.

Fold in peaches. Divide muffin batter into greased muffin pan cups, filling each two-thirds full. Bake muffins 20-25 minutes or until they are golden brown. Cool in pan on wire rack 5 minutes. Remove muffins from pan and serve warm. *Yield: 12 muffins.*

APPLESAUCE MUFFINS

2 C. biscuit mix
¼ C. sugar
1 tsp. ground cinnamon
1 egg, slightly beaten
½ C. applesauce

¼ C. milk
2 T. vegetable oil
¼ C. sugar
½ tsp. ground cinnamon
2 T. butter, melted

Combine biscuit mix, ¼ cup sugar and 1 teaspoon cinnamon in a large bowl. Make a well in center of mixture. Combine egg, applesauce, milk and oil in a small bowl. Add applesauce mixture to dry ingredients, stirring until just moistened.

Spoon batter into greased muffin pan cups, filling two thirds full. Bake at 400° for 12 minutes.

Combine ¼ cup sugar and ½ teaspoon cinnamon in a small bowl. Dip tops of warm muffins in melted butter, then in sugar mixture. *Yield: 12 muffins.*

CHOCOLATE CHIP AND ORANGE MUFFINS

¾ C. milk
½ C. vegetable oil
1 egg
1 tsp. vanilla
2 C. all-purpose flour
⅓ C. firmly packed brown
   sugar

1 T. baking powder
1 tsp. salt
⅔ C. semisweet chocolate
   chips
2 T. grated orange peel

Preheat oven to 400°. Grease ten ½-cup muffin cups. Combine first four ingredients in a bowl. Mix together flour, brown sugar, baking powder and salt. Stir into liquid ingredients. Fold in chocolate chips and orange peel. Divide batter among prepared cups.

Bake until a knife inserted in centers comes out clean, about 20 minutes. Let stand 5 minutes. Remove muffins from cups. Serve warm or at room temperature. *Yield: 10 muffins.*

Hushpuppies

1 ½ C. cornmeal
½ C. flour
1 T. baking powder
½ tsp. baking soda
1 T. salt

2 onions, diced
1 egg
1 C. buttermilk
2 C. cooking oil

Mix dry ingredients and onions. Add egg and buttermilk; let stand for 30 minutes.

Drop ½ tablespoon of mixture into oil heated to 350° in a medium saucepan. (Dip spoon in water before scooping up mixture and it will easily come off the spoon.) Cook 3 5 minutes. Repeat process with remaining batter. *Yield: 3 dozen.*

Note: For a little extra zip, add chopped jalapeno.

CORNBREAD DRESSING

3 C. crumbled cornbread
3 C. herb-seasoned stuffing
1 stick butter
1 large onion, finely chopped
1 C. finely chopped celery

3 C. turkey or chicken broth
  (enough to moisten mixture)
3 eggs, beaten
Salt and pepper to taste

Mix together cornbread crumbs and stuffing; set aside. Melt butter in heavy skillet and sauté onion and celery in butter until translucent. Add broth and pan drippings; pour entire mixture over crumb/seasoning blend.

Work very lightly to blend (working this dressing too much ruins the taste and texture); more broth may be added to adjust to desired moistness. Add beaten eggs and mix lightly; add salt and pepper to taste.

Use part of this dressing for stuffing turkey or other poultry, if desired. Bake remainder in shallow pan for 30 minutes at 350°.
Yield: Dressing for 18-22 pound turkey, with enough left for 8-10 servings.

DESSERTS AND CANDIES

CHRISTMAS AT THE GINGERBREAD HOUSE

Christmas in the Asendorfs' Gingerbread House was truly spectacular. Their Christmas decorations featured candles in every window of the fanciful house. The Christmas tree held a place of honor in the parlor, with the double pocket doors leading to the parlor closed to the children until Christmas morning. Each year Cord Asendorf, Jr., put twinkling lights outside, nestled within the graceful gingerbread arches.

Children in the neighborhood, many of whom used to walk by the Gingerbread House each day on their way to school, have other memories of Papa Asendorf and Christmas. After he retired, Mr. Asendorf could often be seen in his rocking chair on the home's large front porch. Over the years, a legend grew among the neighborhood children that Mr. Asendorf, with his long flowing beard, was Santa Claus in disguise. According to the legend, he spent all year in the Gingerbread House, waiting until Christmas Eve to put on his suit and deliver gifts to Savannah's children.

Although a century has passed since those early holidays, Christmas at the Gingerbread House still features decorations that are reminiscent of those used long ago. Tiny twinkling lights adorn a bountiful Christmas tree, which is covered with hundreds of frilly lace ornaments. Greenery cascades down the staircase, highlighted by beautiful pink bows, and carolers on the sideboard appear ready to burst into 19th-century song. Stepping into the Gingerbread House during the holidays is indeed like stepping back in time.

MENU

Southern Holiday Dinner

Baked Cornish Hens with
Cornbread Dressing

Honey-Glazed Ham

Cashew Rice Pilaf with
Baby Green Peas

Glazed Sweet Potatoes

Green Beans with
Mushrooms and Parmesan

Squash Casserole

Watergate Salad

Peach Cobbler

Pecan Pie

Eggnog

This menu is truly Southern, except for the
Watergate Salad. This sweet salad, more a dessert
than a salad, is a Galloway favorite that has
become a part of our holiday tradition. Serve it as
part of the meal or as a special dessert.

BANANA NUT CAKE

1¾ C. all-purpose flour
¾ C. sugar
1¼ tsp. cream of tartar
¾ tsp. baking soda
½ tsp. salt
2 ripe bananas, mashed

2 eggs, beaten
½ C. vegetable oil
¾ C. chopped pecans
1 pkg. banana pudding mix
Chocolate frosting
Pecans for garnish

Mix by hand. Combine first five ingredients in a large bowl; make a well in the center of the mixture. Combine bananas, eggs, oil and pecans; add to dry ingredients and stir just until moistened.

Pour into a 9" springform pan. Bake 35 minutes at 350° or until toothpick comes out clean. Cool completely.

Prepare banana pudding according to package directions; chill. Cut cake into two layers. Spread pudding on bottom layer, then top with second layer. Frost with chocolate frosting; decorate with pecans. *Yield: 14-16 servings.*

APPLESAUCE CAKE

2½ C. all-purpose flour
2 C. sugar
2 C. applesauce
½ C. vegetable shortening,
   room temperature
½ C. water
2 eggs, lightly beaten
1½ tsp. baking powder
1½ tsp. baking soda
1 tsp. vanilla

1 tsp. salt
1 tsp. cinnamon
½ tsp. ground cloves
½ tsp. ground allspice
½ tsp. grated nutmeg
1 C. chopped pecans
1 C. raisins
Prepared vanilla frosting
   (optional)
Pecan halves (optional)

Preheat oven to 350°. Grease and flour two 9" round baking pans or 2 medium loaf pans. Combine flour, sugar, applesauce, shortening, water, eggs, baking powder, baking soda, vanilla, salt, cinnamon, cloves, allspice and nutmeg in large bowl and beat well. Stir in 1 cup pecans and raisins; turn into pans.

Bake until golden brown and toothpick inserted in center comes out clean, 30-35 minutes; cool completely. Frost round cake layers with vanilla frosting and decorate with pecan halves. Leave loaf cakes unfrosted. *Yield: 10-12 servings.*

FUDGE CAKE

12 oz. semisweet chocolate
5 T. strong coffee
1 C. butter
2 C. sugar

6 egg yolks
1 C. all-purpose flour
6 egg whites
Chocolate Glaze (below)

Preheat oven to 350°. Grease and flour a 9" springform pan. Melt chocolate and coffee in double boiler, then cool; set aside.

Cream together butter and sugar. Add egg yolks, one at a time, to creamed mixture. Add flour.

Beat egg whites until stiff. Add chocolate mixture to egg whites, then fold into butter, egg and flour mixture. Pour into prepared pan and bake 60-70 minutes. When done, top will be crusty and cracked and middle will still be slightly moist. Pour Chocolate Glaze over top of cake. *Yield: 6-8 servings.*

CHOCOLATE GLAZE

4 oz. semisweet chocolate   2 T. butter, melted

Melt chocolate in top of double boiler over hot water. Whisk in melted butter.

Sour Cream Coffee Cake

Topping:
½ C. chopped nuts
1 tsp. cinnamon
2 T. sugar

Cake:
2¼ C. sifted flour
2 tsp. baking powder

½ tsp. baking soda
½ tsp. salt
¾ C. butter, room temperature
1½ C. sugar
2 eggs
1 tsp. vanilla
1 C. sour cream, room
  temperature

Preheat oven to 350°. Grease and flour a 9" tube pan. Prepare topping by combining nuts, cinnamon and 2 tablespoons sugar; set aside. Sift flour; add baking powder, baking soda and salt and set aside.

Cream butter and 1½ cups sugar; add eggs and vanilla. Add flour mixture in 3 portions, alternating with sour cream.

Spread half of batter in pan and sprinkle with half of topping. Spoon on remaining batter and sprinkle with rest of topping. Bake for 45-50 minutes (40 minutes if using an oblong pan). Cool 20 minutes, then remove from pan. *Yield: 12-16 servings.*

MINIATURE CARROT CAKES

1½ C. all-purpose flour
1 tsp. baking powder
1 tsp. baking soda
½ tsp. salt
1 tsp. cinnamon
1 C. sugar
1¾ C. grated carrots
⅔ C. vegetable oil
2 eggs
1 (8¼ oz.) can crushed
 pineapple, drained
1 tsp. vanilla

Cream Cheese Frosting:
1 (3 oz.) pkg. cream cheese,
 softened
¼ C. butter, softened
½ tsp. vanilla
2-2½ C. powdered sugar,
 sifted

In a large bowl, combine first six ingredients; set aside. Mix carrots, oil, eggs, pineapple and 1 teaspoon vanilla; add to dry ingredients and beat 2 minutes with a mixer at medium speed. Pour into greased and floured ½-cup muffin tins. Bake at 350° for 20-25 minutes, or until a toothpick inserted in the center comes out clean. Cool in pan for 5 minutes, then turn out onto a clean, dry surface.

To make frosting, combine cream cheese and butter, mixing well. Add ½ teaspoon vanilla and enough powdered sugar to reach desired consistency. Frost individual cakes with Cream Cheese Frosting. *Yield: 12 miniature cakes.*

Toasted Coconut Pies

2 C. sugar
¼ C. flour
4 large eggs
1 stick butter, melted

2 C. evaporated milk
2 C. coconut
1 tsp. vanilla
2 unbaked pie shells

Mix sugar and flour; add eggs, butter, milk, coconut and vanilla. Mix well; pour into unbaked pie shells. Bake 30-40 minutes at 350° or until set. *Yield: 14-16 servings.*

Note: These can also be made into 3" tarts. Adjust cooking time to 20-25 minutes.

Pecan Pie

3 eggs, beaten
1 C. sugar
¾ C. light corn syrup

¼ C. butter, melted
1 C. pecans, coarsely chopped
1 (9") unbaked pie shell

Mix eggs, sugar and syrup together with an electric mixer. Add melted butter and blend thoroughly.

Sprinkle pecans in bottom of pie shell. Pour egg mixture over nuts. Bake 40-45 minutes in 350° oven. *Yield: 6-8 servings.*

APPLE AND GREEN TOMATO PRESERVE PIE

4 Granny Smith apples, peeled
  and sliced
1 (9 oz.) jar sweet green
  tomato preserves
¼ C. flour

1 prepared 10" pie shell
½ C. sugar
½ C. flour
6 T. cold butter, cut in small
  pieces

Mix apples, green tomato preserves and ¼ cup flour. Pour into unbaked pie shell.

To make crumb topping, mix together sugar, ½ cup flour and butter, then sprinkle on top of pie.

Bake at 350° for 45 50 minutes, or until top is brown and bubbly. Cool before slicing. Makes a delicious sweet-and-sour apple pie.
Yield: 8 servings.

Praline Cheesecake

1¼ C. graham cracker crumbs
¼ C. white sugar
¼ C. finely chopped pecans, toasted
¼ C. butter or margarine, melted
3 (8 oz.) pkgs. cream cheese, softened
1 C. packed brown sugar
1 (5⅓ oz.) can evaporated milk
2 T. all-purpose flour
1½ tsp. vanilla
3 eggs
½ C. pecan halves, toasted
Brown Sugar Sauce (below)

Combine graham cracker crumbs, white sugar and chopped pecans. Stir in butter; press mixture over bottom and sides of a 9" springform pan. Bake in a 350° oven 10 minutes.

In a large bowl, combine cream cheese and 1 cup brown sugar. Add milk, flour and 1½ teaspoons vanilla; beat well. Add eggs; beat until blended.

Pour mixture into crust. Bake at 350° for 50 minutes or until set. Cool 30 minutes; loosen sides, remove rim from pan and cool. Arrange pecan halves over cheesecake. Spoon Brown Sugar Sauce over nuts (recipe follows). *Yield: 16 servings.*

Brown Sugar Sauce

1 C. dark corn syrup
¼ C. cornstarch
2 T. brown sugar
1 tsp. vanilla

Combine syrup, cornstarch and brown sugar in saucepan. Cook and stir until thickened and bubbly; cook and stir 2 minutes more. Remove from heat, stir in 1 teaspoon vanilla, and cool slightly; stir before serving.

CREAM CHEESE BROWNIES

1 (8 oz.) pkg. cream cheese,
   softened
¼ C. sugar
1 tsp. cinnamon
1 egg
1½ tsp. vanilla
1 C. butter
4 (1 oz.) squares unsweetened
   chocolate

2 C. sugar
4 eggs
2 tsp. vanilla
1½ C. self-rising flour (or, add
   ½ tsp. salt if not self-rising)
Chocolate Frosting (below)

Preheat oven to 350°. Combine first five ingredients; beat 2 minutes and set aside. Heat butter and chocolate until melted; cool. Beat chocolate mixture, 2 cups sugar, 4 eggs and 2 teaspoons vanilla at medium speed, about 1 minute. Beat in flour at low speed, about ½ minute. Beat at medium speed 1 minute.

Grease and flour a 9" x 13" pan. Spread half of dough in pan, then cream filling, then rest of batter. Swirl through batter for a marbling effect. Bake 40-45 minutes. Cool and frost with Chocolate Frosting. *Yield: 24 brownies.*

CHOCOLATE FROSTING

3 T. butter, softened
3 T. cocoa
1 T. light corn syrup or honey

½ tsp. vanilla
1 C. powdered sugar
1-2 T. milk

Mix all ingredients together in order given. Milk and powdered sugar quantities can be varied to achieve desired consistency. Spread on brownies; allow to set before cutting brownies.

BAVARIAN CRÈME

1 pt. whipping cream
1 C. (scant) sugar
1 pkg. unflavored gelatin
1 tsp. vanilla

16 oz. sour cream, room
   temperature
1 C. fresh fruit (strawberries,
   blueberries or raspberries)

Mix cream and sugar; sprinkle top with gelatin and whisk into cream and sugar mixture. Heat, stirring constantly, until mixture dissolves; do not boil. Stir in vanilla.

Remove from heat and stir in sour cream. Chill and serve with fresh fruit. *Yield: 6-8 servings.*

FRUIT COMPOTE

½ tsp. grated orange rind
⅔ C. orange juice
½ tsp. grated lemon rind
⅓ C. lemon juice
⅓ C. firmly packed brown
   sugar
1 (3") stick cinnamon

½ tsp. cornstarch
4 oranges
2 C. fresh pineapple
2 kiwifruit
1 C. seedless red grapes
2 C. fresh strawberries, sliced
3 bananas, sliced

In a small saucepan, mix first seven ingredients in order given; cook, stirring, over medium heat until mixture thickens and begins to boil. Set aside.

Section and cut oranges and pineapple into bite-sized pieces; peel and slice kiwifruit. Add red grapes, sliced strawberries and sliced bananas. Pour liquid mixture over fruit and toss gently.
Yield: 8 servings.

Apple Crisp

Juice of 1 lemon
2 C. water
4 large tart apples
    (about 2 lbs.)
½ C. unsweetened apple juice
2 T. white sugar
1 tsp. grated lemon zest
¾ tsp. cinnamon
¼ tsp. ground ginger

Topping:
½ C. rolled oats
3 T. light brown sugar
3 T. all-purpose flour
2 T. butter or margarine

Preheat oven to 375°. Grease a 9" square microwave baking dish. Place lemon juice and water in a bowl. Peel, core and thinly slice apples; drop into lemon water to prevent discoloration.

Drain apples, reserving ¼ cup of lemon water. Toss apples in a bowl with apple juice, reserved lemon water, sugar, lemon zest, cinnamon and ginger. Spoon mixture into baking dish.

Cook in microwave on high for 7 minutes, stirring twice, until apples are tender but not mushy. Remove from microwave.

For topping, combine dry ingredients in a bowl. Cut in butter or margarine with two knives; toss lightly with fingers until mixture resembles coarse meal. Sprinkle topping evenly over apples and bake in preheated oven until bubbly and golden, about 20 minutes. Let rest for 5 minutes before serving. *Yield: 9 servings.*

PEACH COBBLER

Fruit Base:
3 lbs. ripe fresh peaches
1 T. lemon juice
¼ C. firmly packed light brown
   sugar
1½ T. cornstarch
½ C. water

Topping:
½ C. white sugar
½ C. unsifted all-purpose flour
½ tsp. baking powder
¼ tsp. salt
2 T. butter, softened
1 large egg

Preheat oven to 400°. Lightly grease a 2-quart casserole. Peel and slice peaches; place in casserole and stir in lemon juice. In 1-quart saucepan, stir together brown sugar and cornstarch. Gradually add water, stirring until cornstarch is dissolved. Cook over medium heat, stirring constantly until sauce has thickened, about 5 minutes. Pour sauce over peaches in casserole.

To prepare topping, set aside 1 teaspoon white sugar; stir together in medium bowl the remaining white sugar, flour, baking powder and salt. With wooden spoon, stir in butter and egg until a soft dough forms.

Drop topping by spoonfuls onto peach mixture. Sprinkle with reserved 1 teaspoon white sugar. Bake 40-45 minutes or until topping is golden brown and filling is bubbly. Cool slightly. Sprinkle with additional white sugar. Serve warm or at room temperature. *Yield: 8 servings.*

CHEWY OATMEAL COOKIES

½ C. butter
½ C. shortening
1 C. sugar
2 eggs
2 C. flour
2 C. quick oats
1 tsp. baking soda
1 tsp. cinnamon

1 tsp. cloves
½ tsp. salt
½ tsp. nutmeg
1 C. raisins (cooked in ⅓ C. water to make ¼ C. raisin juice)
½ C. chopped walnuts or pecans (optional)

Preheat oven to 350°. Cream butter, shortening, sugar and eggs. Sift dry ingredients together and add to rest of mixture. Add raisin juice; stir in raisins and nuts. Drop by heaping teaspoons onto cookie sheet; bake 12-15 minutes or until done. *Yield: 2 dozen.*

APPLE, OAT AND SESAME COOKIES

1½ C. rolled oats
¾ C. each all-purpose and whole wheat flour
¼ C. sesame seeds
¼ C. packed brown sugar
1½ tsp. baking powder
1½ tsp. cinnamon

¼ tsp. salt
1 C. finely chopped golden delicious apples
½ C. honey
½ C. vegetable oil
1 egg, beaten
⅓ C. milk

Combine oatmeal, flour, sesame seeds, brown sugar, baking powder, cinnamon and salt. Stir apples into dry ingredients. Combine remaining ingredients and add to apple mixture. Drop by spoonfuls onto ungreased cookie sheets. Bake at 375° for 10-12 minutes or until lightly browned. Remove to wire rack and cool. *Yield: 3 dozen.*

SAVANNAH PRALINES

3 C. sugar
Pinch salt
1 C. dark corn syrup

1 C. milk
3 C. nuts, coarsely chopped
1 tsp. vanilla

Put sugar, salt, corn syrup and milk in a saucepan. Beat until creamy. Heat syrup mixture until the sugar dissolves. Add nuts and cook, stirring gently, to the soft-ball stage. Remove mixture from heat and stir in vanilla. Let cool until mixture is lukewarm.

When mixture has cooled, stir pralines again until creamy. Drop ingredients by tablespoon onto waxed paper.
Yield: Approximately 3 dozen.

CREAM CHEESE CHOCOLATE TRUFFLES

4 C. powdered sugar
1 (8 oz.) pkg. cream cheese, softened
1 tsp. vanilla

5 oz. unsweetened chocolate, melted
Toasted almonds, cocoa or coconut for coating

Gradually add powdered sugar to cream cheese, mixing well after each addition. Add vanilla and chocolate; mix well. Chill 1 hour or more.

If using almonds or coconut, chop in food processor until fine. Shape chocolate mixture into ¾" balls; roll in almonds, cocoa, coconut or additional powdered sugar. Chill until ready to serve. *Yield: 4 dozen.*

HOT FUDGE SAUCE

1 (12 oz.) pkg. semisweet
  chocolate chips
½ C. butter

2 C. miniature marshmallows
¾ C. milk

Combine chocolate chips and butter in a double boiler over hot water, stirring until chips have melted. Stir in marshmallows and milk. Cook and stir until marshmallows melt and mixture is smooth.

Serve warm over ice cream, or use as a dipping sauce for fresh fruit. Store unused amount in refrigerator; reheat by microwaving 1 minute for each cup of sauce. *Yield: 4 cups.*

HOLIDAY BOURBON BRANDY BALLS

1 small box vanilla wafers,
  crushed
1½ T. cocoa
2 T. light corn syrup
1 C. powdered sugar

1 C. chopped pecans
¼ C. brandy
¼ C. bourbon
Powdered sugar for coating

Mix all ingredients thoroughly and roll into balls; balls will be quite moist. Sprinkle additional powdered sugar on waxed paper and roll the balls to coat. Store in an airtight container until ready to serve. *Yield: 4 dozen.*

Peanut Butter Balls

½ C. butter
2 C. peanut butter
1 lb. powdered sugar
3 C. crisp rice cereal
1 (8 oz.) milk chocolate bar

1 (6 oz.) pkg. semisweet
  chocolate chips
½ cake (1.6 oz.) canning
  paraffin

Blend butter, peanut butter and powdered sugar. Mix in cereal and roll into ¾" balls. Set aside.

Melt chocolate bar, chips and wax in double boiler. Turn heat to low. Dip balls into chocolate; put on waxed paper and refrigerate. May be frozen. *Yield: 8 dozen.*

Macaroons

¼ C. butter
½ lb. marshmallows (32 large
  marshmallows)
2 T. maple syrup

4 C. corn flakes
½ C. chopped, toasted
  almonds
½ C. mixed candied fruit

In top of double boiler, over hot (not boiling) water, melt butter and marshmallows. Add syrup and stir to mix well.

Combine corn flakes, almonds and candied fruit. Pour hot marshmallow mixture over almond and fruit mixture and toss lightly with a fork to mix thoroughly. Drop by teaspoons onto waxed paper. Let cool. *Yield: Approximately 3 dozen.*

RUGELACH

2 C. all-purpose flour	⅔ C. sugar
1 T. sugar	2 T. ground cinnamon
½ tsp. salt	¼ C. butter, melted
⅔ C. shortening	½ C. raisins
1 egg yolk	½ C. chopped pecans
1 T. grated orange rind	1 egg yolk
⅓ C. orange juice	1 T. water

Combine first three ingredients in a large bowl; cut in shortening with pastry blender until mixture resembles coarse meal. Stir in 1 egg yolk and orange rind, mixing well. Sprinkle orange juice, 1 tablespoon at a time, into flour mixture, stirring until dry ingredients are moistened. Divide dough in half, shape into 2 balls and chill 30 minutes.

Combine ⅔ cup sugar with cinnamon; set aside. Roll half the pastry into a 12" x 10" rectangle. Brush with half the butter; sprinkle half the sugar mixture evenly over pastry. Sprinkle with half the raisins and pecans.

Roll up jelly roll fashion. Pinch seam and ends together; place roll, seam side down, on a lightly greased baking sheet. Repeat procedure with remaining pastry and filling.

Cut each roll into ¾" slices, cutting three fourths of the way through roll from top to bottom. Combine 1 egg yolk and water; brush tops of rolls with mixture. Bake at 350° for 30 minutes or until golden brown. *Yield: 3 dozen.*

MINIATURE CHOCOLATE PEANUT BUTTER PIES

1¼ C. graham cracker crumbs
5 T. unsalted butter, melted
½ C. plus 2 T. sour cream
2½ T. powdered sugar
2 T. whipping cream

½ C. plus 2 T. creamy peanut butter
½ C. whipping cream
4 oz. semisweet chocolate, chopped

Mix graham cracker crumbs and butter in a small bowl. Press crumb mixture on bottom and up the sides of 24 miniature muffin tins. Place in freezer for 20 minutes.

Whisk sour cream, powdered sugar and 2 tablespoons whipping cream in bowl to blend. Add peanut butter and whisk until smooth. Spoon 1 tablespoon peanut butter mixture into each graham cracker crust; freeze 3 hours.

Bring ½ cup whipping cream to simmer in heavy small saucepan. Reduce heat to low; add chocolate and stir until melted. Cool completely, stirring occasionally.

Spoon 2 teaspoons chocolate mixture over each peanut butter pie. Place in freezer until set. Can be prepared 1 week ahead; keep frozen.

To serve, use the tip of a small sharp knife to pry pies carefully from tins. Arrange pies chocolate side up on plate. Let stand 10 minutes at room temperature before serving. *Yield: 24 miniature pies.*

INDEX

INDEX

INDEX

THE GINGERBREAD HOUSE
1921 Bull Street
Savannah, Georgia 31401
(912) 234-7303

Your Order	Qty	Total
The Gingerbread House Cookbook $15.95 per book		$
Georgia residents add 6% sales tax per book		$
Shipping and handling $3.50 per book		$
Total		$

Name

Street Address

City   State   Zip

Phone

Make checks payable to The Gingerbread House.

Photocopies accepted